In honor and memory of:

Mrs. Alice Andersen

Mrs. Martha Chrispin

Mrs. Georgia Deal

Mrs. Val Eggerss

Mrs. Alice George

Mrs. Helen Hoghe

Mrs. Olive Jackson

Mrs. Ruby Riggin

Mrs. Ruth Tomkins

Presented by:
The Van Wert Woman's Club
1998

What Perennial Where

What Perennial Where

ROY LANCASTER

DK PUBLISHING, INC.

A DK PUBLISHING BOOK

EDITOR Anna Cheifetz
ART EDITOR Helen Robson
MANAGING EDITOR Jonathan Metcalf
MANAGING ART EDITOR Peter Cross
US EDITORS Barbara Ellis, Ray Rogers
PRODUCTION MANAGER Michelle Thomas
DTP DESIGNERS Mark Bracey, Robert Campbell

First American Edition, 1997
2 4 6 8 10 9 7 5 3 1
Published in the United States by DK Publishing, Inc.,
95 Madison Avenue, New York, New York 10016
Visit us on the World Wide Web at http://www.dk.com

Lancaster, Roy
What perennial where / Roy Lancaster. – 1st American ed.
p. cm.
Includes index.
ISBN 0-7894-2087-2
1. Perennials. 2. Perennials–Location. I. Title.
SB434.L35 1997
635.9'327–dc21 97-16627
CIP

Text film output by The Right Type, Great Britain. Reproduced by Colourscan, Singapore
Printed and bound in Great Britain by Butler and Tanner, Frome and London

CONTENTS

How This Book Works

In this book, my aim is to help you choose the most suitable perennials for a given garden situation or special ornamental effect, taking the characteristics of different plants and your local growing conditions into consideration. The book is divided into five sections: Soil and Exposure, Specific Uses, Floral Effect, Foliage Effect, and Specialist Plants. Within each section, I give a choice of plants suited to your particular needs and lists of additional planting suggestions. All perennials featured are herbaceous (dying back to below ground level in winter) unless described as evergreen or semievergreen.

What is a Perennial?

I have defined perennials in this book as mainly non-woody plants that live for three years or more. Most are herbaceous, losing their leaves and dying down below ground level, usually in autumn or winter. Some are evergreen, retaining their foliage throughout the winter months. A minority of perennials, including bamboos, have woody stems and evergreen leaves. Subshrubby perennials, such as *Lavatera* and *Perovskia*, are a further group that develop a woody or hardened base. This base may survive low winter temperatures even if the rest of the plant is killed off.

Understanding Hardiness

Hardiness is a measure of a plant's ability to survive and grow under local environmental conditions, especially winter cold. The United States Department of Agriculture has produced a map of the United States divided into 11 hardiness zones based on average annual minimum temperatures recorded from 1974 to 1986. This hardiness map appears on the endpapers of this book. Knowing your region's hardiness zone is a very useful guide and can help you determine if a plant will grow in your garden. However, many other factors, such as summer heat and humidity, soil fertility and drainage, and protection from strong winds, also influence plant hardiness. Many plants will grow beyond their listed hardiness zones if they are provided with extra winter protection, or if other care is taken to modify their environment.

• **Botanical and Common Plant Names**
Below each plant's botanical name is the common name or, if none exists, the generic name.

• **Light Level, Hardiness, and Acidity**
Symbols for light level and hardiness are given for all plants; if a plant requires acid soil, a pH symbol will appear (see boxes for key to symbols).

Perennials with Strap- or Sword-shaped Leaves

Perennials that form clumps of long, slender leaves are irresistible and always striking. Regardless of whether the leaves stand stiff and upright, or bend and arch in a more graceful manner, they are invaluable for contrasting with more conventional, broad-leaved perennials in beds or borders. They can also be used as dramatic specimen plants.

Arundo donax 'Macrophylla'
Giant Reed
☼ 5-9 ↕15ft (5m) ↔6ft (2m)
This giant grass produces long, arching, slender, glaucous leaves and bamboolike stems that flaunt feathery plumes in summer. It prefers a warm, sheltered site.

Eryngium agavifolium
Eryngium
☼ 7-9 ↕4ft (1.2m) ↔24in (60cm)
The sharply toothed, glossy, evergreen leaves form a striking, erect clump above which sturdy stems carry cylindrical heads of tiny, greenish white flowers in summer.

Iris pseudacorus 'Variegata'
Yellow Flag
☼ ☀ 4-9 ↕↔
A vigorous iris for wet sites formir patch of tall green leaves with bol or creamy yellow bands. Yellow flc are borne on erect stems during su

Evergreen and Semieverg Perennials with Strap- or Sword-shaped Leaves
Acorus gramineus
Crocosmia paniculata
Eryngium eburneum, see p.22
Eryngium pandanifolium
Hemerocallis aurantiaca
Iris foetidissima 'Variegata', see p
Watsonia pillansii
Yucca filamentosa
Yucca recurvifolia

Foliage Effect

Crocosmia 'Lucifer'
Crocosmia
☼ ☀ 5-9 ↕4ft (1.2m) ↔18in (45cm)
A bright and cheerful perennial forming a clump of robust, sword-shaped leaves. Its arching, branched spikes of brilliant red, late-summer flowers are good for cutting.

Hemerocallis 'Gentle Shepherd'
Daylily
☼ ☀ 4-9 ↕26in (65cm) ↔4ft (1.2m)
Bold clumps of semievergreen, narrow, arching green leaves are topped by ivory-white, trumpet-shaped flowers with green throats during summer.

Iris sibirica 'Perry's Blue'
Iris
☼ ☀ 2-9 ↕4ft (1.2m)
Erect clumps of narrow, grasslike l are topped by blue-violet flowers soldierlike stems in early summer. winter seed capsules are also deco

116

• **Plant Description**
Gives features of interest such as flowering time, distinctive traits, and preferred sites or conditions.

Key to pH Acidity Symbol

The majority of plants will grow in most soils. Those that require acid soil are highlighted with this symbol.

PH ▼	*Requires acid soil*

Key to Light Level Symbols

Light preferences are shown with the following symbols; more than one indicates a range of tolerance.

☼	*Full sun – prefers, or even requires, as much sun as possible.*
◐	*Partial shade – tolerant of (some even prefer) limited or indirect sunlight.*
☀	*Shade – will grow in a site receiving low light, such as under a tree canopy.*

Plant Names

Currently accepted botanical species and cultivar names are used throughout this book. Common names in general use are given, and where none exists, the generic name is repeated, or else an English name common to the whole genus or group (such as "pinks") is given. Both botanical and common names are indexed.

Plant Dimensions

Plant dimensions vary depending on growing conditions. Sizes are a guide to mature size in average conditions. The height includes flower stems, when appropriate.

↕	*Average height*
↔	*Average spread*
↕↔	*Average height and spread*

Soil & Exposure

To help you choose perennials suited to the conditions in your garden, this section suggests small, medium-, and tall-growing plants for a range of different soil types and light conditions: *Heavy clay soil, Sandy/well-drained soil, Acid soil, Alkaline soil, Dry soil in sun or shade, Moist soil in sun or shade, Warm sheltered sites.*

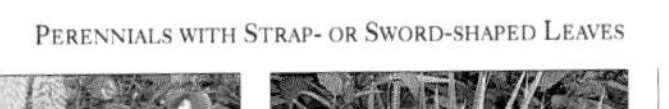

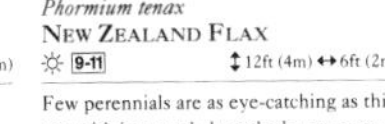

• **Height and Spread**
Gives the average ultimate size of the plant, in imperial and metric.

• **Thumb Marker**
Identifies each of the five sections in the book (see right).

• **Other Plants**
Lists more plants suitable for the site or effect (see box below left).

Other Plant Suggestions

On each spread, boxes provide additional lists of perennials suitable for the site or effect with page references given for those illustrated in other sections. Where a listed genus is followed by "spp. and cvs.," this indicates that many or all of the species and cultivars in this genus may be suitable for use in your garden's hardiness zone.

Specific Uses

This section suggests perennials for specific garden sites: *Rock gardens, Bog gardens and waterside areas, Wild margins or along hedges*; for specific uses: *Naturalizing, Cut flowers or foliage, Seedheads, Containers, Flowers attractive to bees and butterflies*; and for tolerance of: *Exposed sites, Air pollution, Rabbits, Deer, Slugs and snails.*

Floral Effect

For flowers throughout the year and for different uses or effects, this section suggests perennials in the following categories: *Long flowering season*; *Spring, Early to midsummer, Mid- to late summer, Autumn, or Winter flowering*; *Flowers borne in sprays and flattened heads, or spikes*; *Hot-, Cool-, or Pale-colored flowers*; *Fragrant flowers.*

Foliage Effect

Foliage forms the basis of any garden. Perennials in this section are grouped by their leaf type: *Bold, Evergreen, Strap- or sword-shaped, Deep-cut or jagged, Feathery, Spiny, Aromatic, Yellow- or gold-variegated, White- or cream-variegated, Gold, Silver or gray-blue, Purple, red, or bronze, Richly tinted in autumn, Decorative in winter.*

Specialist Plants

Some perennials are particularly sought after for their form, foliage, or flowers. This section includes families of perennials that are often collected by enthusiasts: *Geraniums, Hostas, Snowdrops, Hellebores, Epimediums, Peonies.* Some of these plant groups also make excellent specimen plants: *Bamboos, Small grasses and sedges, Large grasses, Ferns.*

Soil & Exposure
Specific Uses
Floral Effect
Foliage Effect
Specialist Plants

INTRODUCTION

PERENNIALS FOUND GROWING WILD – in meadows, forests, and coastal or mountainous areas all over the world – have long made valuable contributions to our gardens. The most varied and versatile of plants, they are easy to grow and will bring year-round attractions of foliage and flowers to gardens of any size and situation.

Coreopsis 'Moonbeam' for pale-coloured flowers

△ AUTHOR'S GARDEN *Many perennials flourish alongside shrubs and trees in my own garden in Hampshire, England.*

The earliest images I have of garden perennials are the ragged blue heads of perennial cornflowers (*Centaurea montana*) growing in my grandfather's garden when I was a boy. Little did I know then that one day, not only would I travel through the world's wild places in search of native plants, but I would also make gardening my career. In the years since, I have come to recognize and know perennials in the wild in a variety of situations, from mountain woods and meadows to prairies, swamps, and coastal plains. Seeing them in their natural habitats where they choose to grow, as well as in our gardens where we want them to grow, has taught me a lot about their requirements, their preferences, and their huge garden potential. Contrary to what we

WHY GROW PERENNIALS?

Variety and versatility are the two main benefits that perennials bring to the garden. There isn't a single garden site in which perennials of some kind cannot be grown. Used with shrubs and trees to build a coherent garden structure, they can provide ground cover, form the bulk of border plants, or fill containers. They offer gardeners year-round color and interest with their vast range of foliage and flower effects, seedheads, and scents. Most are easily cultivated in temperate regions, and can be increased by sowing seed, taking cuttings, or division.

Helleborus argutifolius for evergreen leaves

◁ NATURAL HABITAT *Perennials in the wild give us a number of clues about how we can best use them in our gardens and may also inform and inspire our choice of garden design. This alpine meadow in China's Yunnan province contains many perennials that can be grown in a sunny rock garden in cultivation.*

might expect, the situations and soils in which perennials are found in the wild are not always those that they demand in the garden, although they do offer us some important basic guidelines.

ADAPTABLE AND VERSATILE

Most perennials are surprisingly adaptable in cultivation and will happily tolerate a wide variety of conditions, with only the inevitable exceptions to this rule, such as those requiring acid soil, calling for any special attention. Temperature requirements are another matter, however, for it stands to reason that those perennials growing naturally in warm climates, especially those that enjoy hot, sunny, well-drained conditions, will not thrive in cold gardens where the sun rarely visits. Nevertheless, many enterprising gardeners in such situations have devised ways of circumventing the problem, taking advantage of sheltered corners to grow tender or exotic perennials, or planting them in containers that can be moved indoors in the autumn to carry them over the winter.

IN THE GARDEN

In my own garden in Hampshire, England, on a soil that is mainly sandy and well-drained, I grow hundreds of perennials as well as trees and shrubs. Drawing on this practical experience of perennials in cultivation, combined with observations of plants in the wild, I have tried in *What Perennial Where* to suggest some of the best plants for given soils and situations and to supply information on their merits. If this book helps you grow a plant where once there was nothing, then I shall have succeeded.

△ ATTRACTIVE GROUNDCOVER *Many low-growing or mat-forming perennials make ideal groundcovers. Often thriving in shade, they are also ideal for softening the edges of borders, paths, or steps, or for underplanting beneath shrubs and trees.*

▽ BRIGHT BORDER *Still one of the most popular uses of perennials in the garden, the herbaceous border, devised in the late 19th century, formally arranges plants by height, and often by flower color.*

Designing with Perennials

COLOR, FORM, AND TEXTURE all play an important role in garden design, and perennials offer the widest choice of these ingredients. A designed garden may include particular elements, such as water or paving, or feature a certain mood, color, or theme, such as attracting butterflies. By knowing which perennials are best suited to your garden design, they can be used creatively to enhance any scheme.

Climate, available space, soil, and exposure are all factors that may influence your choice of garden design and the plants best suited to your needs. In most situations there is a huge range of perennials to choose from for optimum effect, although problem sites, like boggy areas, coastal gardens, or clay soil, will all require at least some specialized plants tolerant of such conditions. It is worth remembering that form and foliage are just as important as flowers – if not more so. They provide the garden with a firm basis on which to build and also establish a long-lasting backdrop for whatever flowers briefly appear. While many perennials have tinted leaves in autumn, there are others that have the advantage of a longer display of variegated, colored, or even evergreen foliage.

PERENNIAL PLANTING

With the exception of groundcover plantings and some formal designs, it is vital to maintain enough space between perennials grown in beds and borders. This allows for expansion and also the possibility of self-sown seedlings, which may even result in new forms or hybrids. Group plants that enjoy similar growing conditions together, and

△ MIXED TUB *Containers are ideal for patios or small gardens where space is at a premium. Perennials with attractive leaves, like* Houttuynia, Heuchera, *and* Tolmiea, *are striking and long lasting.*

▷ GRAND DESIGNS *The spectacular borders of landscaped gardens are a good source of ideas. Height or color contrasts are easy to repeat on a smaller scale.*

▽ TEXTURE AND COLOR *The different habits, foliage, and flowers of* Melissa, Linaria, *and* Geranium *'Johnson's Blue' create a vibrant and informal display.*

△ COLOR SPECTRUM *It is possible to achieve impressive effects without using a vast array of perennials. Different forms of the same or similar plants, as in this* Sedum *border, can be planted together to make a bold display.*

△ NATURAL PLANTING *Drifts of grasses and other perennials create an informal effect in this border, inspired by plants in the wild. This increasingly popular style of gardening uses plants appropriate to the site for a low-maintenance approach.*

select perennials best suited to the soil and exposure of your garden to ensure strong, healthy growth and easy management.

GARDEN DESIGNS

Large, landscaped gardens show the scope for spectacular design and the wealth of planting possible where space is no object. However, if scale and contrast are taken into consideration, the grand herbaceous perennial borders often found in these settings can inspire gardeners of even the smallest plots. Small groups of compact plants can easily be combined to recreate the foliage or flowering effects seen in larger beds. Alternatively, try using a single large plant as a highlight. Containers are also a useful option, particularly for small gardens, back-yards, or patios. Bamboos, ferns, and many other foliage and flowering perennials are ideal for containers, and there is a good selection of shade-lovers that will thrive even in sunless areas near to the house.

The "plantsman's garden," where individual plants take precedence over rigid design, will appeal to those gardeners wanting to collect plants in a favorite genus of perennials. While plant variety is the most important consideration here, careful planning of paths and beds will help you cope more easily with the garden's contents.

NATURAL EFFECTS

"Wild" plantings look to perennials growing in their natural habitats for inspiration. Where space allows, the effect of a natural woodland, pond, or meadow can be recreated in the garden environment. Variety is not of prime importance in the wild garden, and large numbers of a few key perennials can be planted in sweeping drifts, naturalized in isolation, or underplanted beneath trees or shrubs. The plants chosen must be tolerant of competition, especially if planted in grass or shade. For this reason, many bulbs along with robust clump-forming or fast-creeping perennials are ideal for this purpose.

An increasingly popular variation on the wild garden is "natural" planting. This involves planting whole borders or beds with loose drifts of perennials, including ornamental grasses. There is no place here for the ordered blocks and tight groups of plants found in more formal designs, as these natural-style borders emulate the effects found in prairies and meadows in the wild. Depending on your taste, or on the size of your garden, it is possible to incorporate just a few grasses into a compact border of perennials or, in larger gardens where space is no object, to create wilder, more naturalistic sweeps of plants. Part of the success of this style of planting is that it uses perennials appropriate to the chosen site. The result is a low-maintenance, wildlife-friendly garden where plants will thrive and care for themselves with less need for intervention such as staking, watering, or pest control.

FACTORS TO CONSIDER WHEN DESIGNING WITH PERENNIALS

Light Where and when shade occurs in your garden is critical as this affects your choice of perennials for different sites. Many perennials tolerate shade; others need all the sun they can get.

Hardiness Give priority to perennials best suited to your local conditions. In colder regions, tender or more exotic perennials may survive in warm, sheltered pockets or in containers.

Color and texture Flowers are the most obvious providers of color in the garden, but often appear only briefly. Perennials with attractive foliage offer valuable texture and drama as well as year-round interest.

Structure Exploit diversity in growth habits and plant size to give structure to formal elements, such as herbaceous borders, or to fulfil specific functions such as ground cover or screening.

Naturalizing Many perennials (bulbs especially) are spectacular planted in drifts for natural effect, particularly in wild, marginal areas. Use them also beneath deciduous shrubs or roses.

Additional uses Many perennials have imposing foliage and flowerheads, some good for cutting, which make them ideal specimen plants. They can also be used to complement walls, paths, or other architectural features.

Perennials through the Seasons

EACH SEASON brings new features and its own particular character to the garden landscape. Perennials mirror this seasonal passage by offering continual changes in growth, foliage, and flowers. While spring and summer are often considered to be the high points of the gardening calendar, with careful planning, even in cold climates perennials can provide nearly year-round interest and colorful or dramatic effects, with one plant taking over as another starts to fade.

PERENNIALS ATTRACTIVE FOR TWO OR MORE SEASONS

Festuca glauca
Geranium spp. and cvs.
Helleborus x *hybridus*, see p.84
Heuchera spp. and cvs.
Lamium galeobdolon 'Hermann's Pride', see p.35
Lavandula angustifolia
Miscanthus sinensis
Polystichum spp. and cvs.
Pulmonaria spp. and cvs.
Sasa veitchii, see p.135
Sedum 'Herbstfreude', see p.73
Vinca minor

Seasonal changes in the garden are reflected most clearly in flowering and foliage displays. While some perennials flower for a relatively brief period, their spectacular blooms may be long remembered and eagerly looked forward to in subsequent years. Perennials with extended flowering periods (often spanning several months) provide strong links between the seasons, and their contribution can be relied upon year after year. This is particularly important in smaller gardens, where each plant must contribute the maximum amount of color and interest. Perennials with attractive foliage will provide an even longer season of interest, and can be invaluable where space is limited. While herbaceous plants often have richly tinted leaves in autumn, it is worth growing some of the many perennials that have evergreen or semievergreen foliage. Those with variegated or brightly colored leaves are also useful.

SPRING

The re-emergence of herbaceous perennials in spring is, for many gardeners, one of the most exciting events in the year. Rootstocks that have lain below ground all through winter now send out strong, and sometimes brightly colored, new shoots. Since many trees and shrubs begin growing in late spring, perennials provide much of the first garden color of the new year. Bulbs will bring welcome early blooms and are excellent for planting in groups, naturalizing in large drifts, or underplanting beneath trees or shrubs. Tulips, daffodils, and many

△ SPRING CONTAINER *Bulbs, like these daffodils, are ideal for naturalizing or for tubs. They are a useful source of early color in the garden, providing a rich variety of spring flower effects.*

▷ SUMMER BORDER *Perennials can bring a blaze of color to the garden during the summer months. In this border, the bright blooms of delphiniums, lupines,* Anthemis, Oenothera, *and* Geranium psilostemon *compete with a multitude of other plants for attention.*

△ EARLY WINTER *After flowering, many perennials produce decorative seedheads. These can provide enchanting effects when touched with frost or snow, a bonus that tidy-minded gardeners often forfeit.*

◁ AUTUMN COLOR *The richly tinted foliage of* Geranium macrorrhizum *is a striking backdrop for colchicums in autumn. The leaf color will continue to develop after the flowers have faded.*

other bulbs can also provide some of the first cut flowers of the year, and will thrive in containers in a patio or backyard.

SUMMER

After the initial rush of spring flowers, the garden settles down to a more leisurely pace. Many of the most popular perennials, such as yarrow (*Achillea*), shasta daisies, and other members of the huge daisy family are at their best now. Long-flowering perennials, like sundrops (*Oenothera*), bloom through summer and even into autumn. Summer is also the time when perennials with a stately habit or bold foliage attain their ultimate size, stamping their presence on the garden scene. In regions where summers are dry, it is worth growing perennials such as sea hollies (*Eryngium*) and yuccas, which tolerate sun and little water.

AUTUMN

Perennials with late flowers, fruits, or richly tinted foliage can make autumn one of the most colorful seasons, despite its place at the end of the growing year. Autumn bulbs, such as colchicums and dwarf cyclamen, flower alongside golden rod (*Solidago*) and asters. Foliage can also make an important contribution – the dying leaves of herbaceous perennials such as many hardy geraniums providing brilliant tints of purple, yellow, and red. Showy seedheads, often good for cutting, add to the display. Wise gardeners will also use ornamental grasses, like the fountain grass (*Pennisetum alopecuroides*), to add interest to borders or containers. In addition to their bold form and foliage, many of these grasses have striking seedheads that will last into winter.

WINTER

The winter months are often least liked by gardeners, but this does not have to be a featureless time when the garden is either ignored or avoided. Gardeners in warmer zones can choose from the many perennials that have attractive semi-evergreen or evergreen foliage, some of it brightly colored. These foliage plants, invaluable in their own right, will also provide an attractive setting for late-winter to early spring-flowering hellebores, as well as for snowdrops and other similar miniature bulbs that signal the oncoming spring. Perennials whose dried seedheads or superstructures survive through autumn and into winter will provide further dramatic interest in the garden.

▷ LATE WINTER *Use perennials to bring warmth and color to the garden from late winter to early spring. Here, snowdrops grow with* Bergenia *'Bressingham Ruby'.*

SOIL & EXPOSURE

THE TYPE OF SOIL found in your garden and how much sun or shade it enjoys are two of the most critical factors to consider when selecting plants for your plot. While many perennials are flexible in their needs, tolerating a range of garden situations, they can be used to better effect if you are aware of their preferences.

Anemonopsis macrophylla for moist soil in shade

Soils vary considerably in their physical and chemical nature. While most perennials thrive in what is commonly called average or "moist but well-drained" soil, which retains enough moisture to satisfy a plant's needs without becoming waterlogged, some have much more specific requirements. Look at the color and texture of your soil and use the soil panel (*right*) to establish which type of soil you have.

All plants require some sunlight to survive, but while some demand full sun for top performance, others tolerate, or even prefer, varying degrees of shade. Many perennials thrive in the partial shade cast by buildings, walls, or light-canopied deciduous trees, like birch, or under shallow-rooted trees like maples. A more careful choice is needed for sites in the heavy shade that occurs beneath dense tree canopies.

Perennials in this section are grouped according to their soil and lighting needs to provide planting solutions for a range of garden sites.

SOIL GUIDE

The clay, sand, or silt particles in your garden soil will dictate its physical and chemical make-up. It may be heavy (wet and poorly drained) or light (dry and free-draining). Acidity or alkalinity (pH value) is measured on a scale of 1 to 14. Below neutral (7), soils are acid; above neutral they are alkaline.

AVERAGE *soil suits the widest range of plants. Slightly acid or neutral, it is moist but well-drained.*

HEAVY CLAY *soil can be very fertile, but its tiny particles make it slow-draining if wet and hard-baked if dry.*

SANDY *soil has large particles and is light and free-draining. It often loses nutrients and water quickly.*

RICH *soil is high in nutrients and organic matter. Dark in color, it retains moisture but drains freely.*

POOR *soil can be improved by adding organic matter to increase its fertility and neutralize pH.*

△ SHADY BORDER *Many perennials, like these hostas and irises, enjoy a partially shady site, especially if the soil is moist.*

◁ SUNNY CORNER *Make use of warm, sheltered sites and corners to grow sun-loving, or more exotic tender perennials.*

▷ DRY GARDEN *These striking sedums, sea hollies, and ornamental grasses will thrive in full sun and well-drained soil.*

Low to Medium Perennials for Heavy Clay Soil

HEAVY CLAY SOILS are often wet and sticky in winter, but hard and lumpy in dry summers. When amended with organic matter and mulched, they can also be very fertile and amenable for a wide range of perennials. None of the following will grow much above 36in (90cm) and are suited to small gardens or the front of larger borders and beds.

OTHER LOW TO MEDIUM GROWERS FOR HEAVY CLAY SOIL

Anemone x *hybrida* and cvs.
Aster novi-belgii and cvs.
Astilbe spp. and cvs.
Astrantia major
Brunnera macrophylla, see p.78
Polemonium caeruleum
Primula denticulata
Prunella grandiflora
Stachys macrantha, see p.93
Veronica gentianoides

Ajuga reptans 'Multicolor'
BUGLEWEED
☀ 3-9 ↕6in (15cm) ↔36in (90cm)

This bugleweed forms a mat of creeping stems and bronze-green leaves splashed pink and cream. Short spikes of deep blue flowers are produced in early summer.

Aster x *frikartii* 'Mönch'
FRIKART'S ASTER
☼ 5-8 ↕28in (70cm) ↔16in (40cm)

Reliable displays of large, long-lasting, lavender-blue daisies top strong stems in late summer and autumn. Well worth growing although it may require support.

Campanula takesimana
BELLFLOWER
☼ ☀ 5-8 ↕20in (50cm) ↔3ft (1m)

Reliable on clay soils, this suckering plant has erect stems and heart-shaped leaves. Nodding white bells, pink-flushed and spotted inside, are borne during summer.

Aquilegia vulgaris 'Nora Barlow'
EUROPEAN COLUMBINE
☼ ☀ 3-9 ↕36in (90cm) ↔18in (45cm)

In spring and early summer, tall, upright stems bear showers of nodding, double red pompon flowers with pale green tips above a mound of divided, grayish leaves.

Bergenia crassifolia
BERGENIA
☼ ☀ 3-8 ↕↔18in (45cm)

A tough perennial developing a mound of bold, leathery, semievergreen leaves. In late winter and early spring, reddish stems carry dark pink flowers above the foliage.

Hemerocallis 'Stella de Oro'
DAYLILY
☼ 3-9 ↕24in (60cm) ↔18in (45cm)

Clusters of bright golden yellow flowers open in succession from early summer to fall above dense clumps of strap-shaped leaves. Long-blooming and very reliable.

Hosta 'June'
HOSTA
3-9 ↕16in (40cm) ↔28in (70cm)

This beautiful foliage plant is a sport of the lovely *H.* 'Halcyon'. It has fleshy, long-pointed, yellow-splashed leaves and bears lavender flowers during summer.

Lamium orvala
LAMIUM
4-8 ↕↔20in (50cm)

The nettle-shaped, softly-hairy leaves form a bold, non-invasive clump. Whorls of two-lipped, pinkish purple flowers are produced from late spring into summer.

Prunella grandiflora 'Loveliness'
SELF-HEAL
5-8 ↕6in (15cm) ↔12in (30cm)

A mat-forming, semievergreen perennial with erect stems bearing whorled heads of two-lipped, soft pink flowers in summer. It makes an excellent groundcover.

Paeonia 'Laura Dessert'
PEONY
2-8 ↕30in (75cm) ↔24in (60cm)

During late spring, large, fragrant, double blooms with white, pink-flushed outer petals and creamy yellow centers emerge above a clump of deeply divided leaves.

Ranunculus aconitifolius 'Flore Pleno'
DOUBLE BUTTERCUP
5-9 ↕24in (60cm) ↔18in (45cm)

This clump-forming perennial produces beautiful, deeply lobed leaves and bears branched stems of double white button-like flowers in spring and early summer.

Rudbeckia fulgida var. *sullivantii* 'Goldsturm'
3-9 ↕24in (60cm) ↔18in (45cm)

This colorful perennial has golden yellow daisy flowers with dark centers from late summer into autumn. It performs best with moist but well-drained conditions.

Medium to Tall Perennials for Heavy Clay Soil

MANY OF THE MORE ROBUST perennials are tolerant of heavy clay soils. Some have densely fibrous rootstocks, others are deep-rooted, allowing them to survive as long as their site is not waterlogged. The following perennials, all 3–6ft (1–2m) tall, will do even better if drainage can be improved by adding organic matter, like compost, to the soil.

Aconitum x *cammarum* 'Bicolor'
MONKSHOOD
3-7 ↕4ft (1.2m) ↔24in (60cm)

This stout perennial has deeply divided, sharply toothed, dark green leaves and bears branched heads of helmet-shaped, blue and white flowers during summer.

Centaurea macrocephala
GLOBE CENTAUREA
2-8 ↕4ft (1.2m) ↔36in (90cm)

Throughout summer, this striking, clump-forming perennial produces large, chunky heads of golden yellow flowers with shiny brown bracts atop erect, leafy stems.

Delphinium 'Emily Hawkins'
DELPHINIUM
3-7 ↕5½ft (1.7m) ↔24in (60cm)

No perennial border on clay soil should be without a delphinium. This one bears neat spikes of semidouble, light violet flowers during summer with fawn-colored eyes.

Aruncus dioicus
GOAT'S BEARD
3-7 ↕6ft (2m) ↔4ft (1.2m)

An impressive perennial that forms a bold clump of large, much-divided, fernlike leaves with equally attractive plumes of frothy, creamy white flowers in summer.

Cimicifuga simplex 'Scimitar'
KAMCHATKA BUGBANE
3-8 ↕6ft (2m) ↔24in (60cm)

A handsome perennial with tall, branched spikes of tiny white flowers that rise over the large, bold clumps of deeply divided, fernlike leaves during autumn.

Eupatorium purpureum 'Atropurpureum'
3-8 ↕7ft (2.2m) ↔4ft (1.2m)

A clump-forming native plant with tall, purplish, leafy stems bearing domed heads of pink-purple flowers, loved by bees and butterflies, during summer and autumn.

Helianthus 'Capenoch Star'
PERENNIAL SUNFLOWER
☼ ☀ 5-9 ↕5ft (1.5m) ↔36in (90cm)

The sharply toothed leaves of this bold, clump-forming plant are joined in summer and autumn by branched heads of large, lemon yellow, dark-centered daisies.

Heliopsis helianthoides subsp. *scabra* 'Light of Loddon'
☼ ☀ 3-9 ↕3½ft (1.1m) ↔36in (90cm)

Erect, stout, stiff-branching, leafy stems produce a regular display of semidouble, bright yellow flowerheads with domed centers throughout summer and autumn.

OTHER MEDIUM TO TALL PERENNIALS FOR CLAY SOIL

Anemone x *hybrida*
Aster novae-angliae
Campanula lactiflora 'Loddon Anna', see p.28
Helenium autumnale
Helianthus salicifolius
Macleaya x *kewensis*
Rheum palmatum
Sanguisorba canadensis
Solidago spp. and cvs.

Persicaria amplexicaulis 'Firetail'
PERSICARIA
☼ ☀ 5-9 ↕4ft (1.2m) ↔36in (90cm)

A striking and reliable border perennial with dense clumps of leafy stems bearing long, arching, slender spikes of bright red flowers from summer into autumn.

Rodgersia aesculifolia
RODGERSIA
☼ ☀ 4-7 ↕5½ft (1.7m) ↔36in (90cm)

This lovely rodgersia produces a clump of long-stalked, toothed, coppery-colored leaves topped by eye-catching plumes of creamy white flowers during summer.

Silphium perfoliatum
CUP PLANT, PRAIRIE DOCK
☼ ☀ 3-8 ↕8ft (2.5m) ↔3ft (1m)

Branched heads of yellow daisies adorn this statuesque native plant from summer to autumn. The coarsely toothed upper leaves have fused stalks that form cups.

Low to Medium Perennials for Sandy/Well-drained Soil

There are numerous perennials less than 3ft (1m) in height that are suitable for well-drained soils, especially for sites in full sun. These small to medium-size plants have a multitude of uses, particularly at the front of borders, in raised beds, or along the tops of walls. Some are also ideal for growing in containers on patios or paved areas.

Acanthus hirsutus
Bear's-breech
☼ ☀ 8-10 ↕↔ 12in (30cm)

This low, suckering perennial forms a clump of deeply cut, weakly spiny leaves. During summer, upright, greenish white flower spikes emerge from prickly bracts.

Artemisia 'Powis Castle'
Artemisia
☼ 5-8 ↕ 24in (60cm) ↔ 36in (90cm)

The handsome, filigree, silver-gray foliage of this plant is hard to beat. It forms a low, neat mound, eventually becoming woody and untidy, when it should be replaced.

Diascia 'Joyce's Choice'
Diascia
☼ 7-9 ↕ 10in (25cm) ↔ 20in (50cm)

A free-flowering diascia forming a mat or carpet of trailing stems and small leaves topped throughout summer and autumn by loose sprays of apricot flowers.

Eriophyllum lanatum
Woolly Sunflower
☼ 5-8 ↕↔ 20in (50cm)

This vigorous clump-former has woolly, silver-gray leaves and bears a succession of bright yellow daisy flowers from late spring into summer. It is drought tolerant.

Agapanthus 'Midnight Blue'
African Lily
☼ 8-10 ↕ 18in (45cm) ↔ 12in (30cm)

In summer, fleshy stems carry loose heads of dark blue, trumpet-shaped flowers over clumps of strap-shaped, dark green leaves. Grow in containers in northern gardens.

Borago pygmaea
Borago
☼ 5-9 ↕↔ 24in (60cm)

Loosely branched stems rise from rosettes of leaves to bear nodding, pale blue, bell-shaped flowers over a long period from late spring to autumn. A short-lived plant.

Eryngium bourgatii
Mediterranean Sea Holly
☼ 5-8 ↕ 18in (45cm) ↔ 12in (30cm)

Small blue flowerheads with collars of spine-tipped bracts emerge in summer on branching stems. The spiny, silver-veined, deeply divided leaves form rosettes.

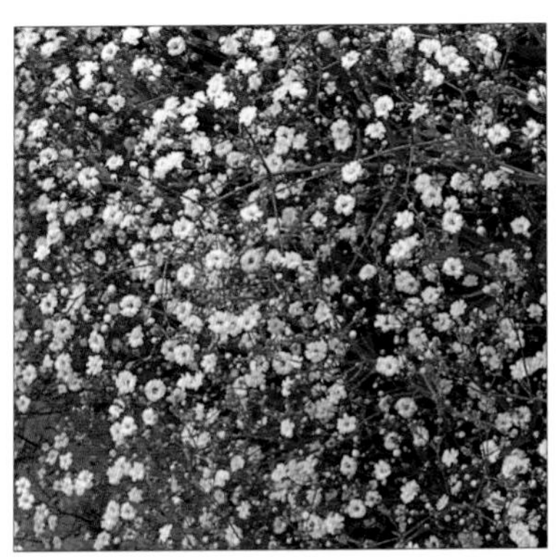

Gypsophila 'Rosenschleier'
BABY'S-BREATH
☼ 3-9 ↕16in (40cm) ↔3ft (1m)

The pretty carpet of bluish green leaves is peppered in summer with tiny, double white flowers that later turn pale pink. It is also known as *G.* 'Rosy Veil'.

Limonium latifolium 'Violetta'
SEA LAVENDER
☼ 3-9 ↕24in (60cm) ↔18in (45cm)

This sea lavender forms a bold rosette of large, dark green leaves. Branched heads of tiny, deep blue-violet late-summer flowers are good for cutting and drying.

Linum narbonense
NARBONNE FLAX
☼ 5-9 ↕20in (50cm) ↔18in (45cm)

During summer, the clump of slender, wiry stems, clothed in narrow, blue-green leaves, is covered by a mass of short-lived, small, deep blue flowers with white eyes.

Oenothera speciosa 'Rosea'
SHOWY EVENING PRIMROSE
☼ 5-8 ↕↔12in (30cm)

The mound of narrow leaves is decorated by saucer-shaped, pale pink blooms with yellow and white centers from summer to autumn. Free-flowering but invasive.

OTHER LOW TO MEDIUM GROWERS FOR SANDY/WELL-DRAINED SOIL

Acanthus dioscoridis, see p.26
Achillea tomentosa
Anagallis monellii
Calamintha nepeta
Centranthus ruber, see p.86
Dianthus deltoides, see p.100
Dictamnus albus, see p.108
Euphorbia nicaeensis, see p.76
Gaillardia x *grandiflora*, see p.68
Geranium malviflorum
Iris innominata
Lavandula angustifolia
Lychnis coronaria
Opuntia humifusa
Sedum spp. and cvs.
Silene polypetala
Solidago sempervirens
Yucca spp. and cvs.

Origanum laevigatum 'Herrenhausen'
OREGANO
☼ 5-9 ↕20in (50cm) ↔18in (45cm)

Bees and butterflies love this plant. The stiffly erect stems, crowded with aromatic leaves, are topped by dense heads of rich pink flowers in summer and autumn.

Medium to Tall Perennials for Sandy/Well-drained Soil

GARDENERS WHO HAVE ADMIRED the lavender-blue spires of a *Perovskia* or a mound of *Crambe cordifolia* in bloom may already know how well these two, and other similar perennials, thrive in well-drained soil, especially in sunny sites. The following, mostly 3–6ft (1–2m) tall, also enjoy such conditions, and will bring presence to a border or bed.

OTHER MEDIUM TO TALL GROWERS FOR SANDY SOIL

Acanthus mollis Latifolius Group
Cortaderia selloana 'Sunningdale Silver', see p.139
Eryngium yuccifolium
Euphorbia characias subsp. *wulfenii*
Liatris aspera
Salvia interrupta
Silene regia
Silene virginica
Solidago odora

Asphodeline lutea
KING'S SPEAR
☼ 6-9 ↕ 5ft (1.5m) ↔ 12in (30cm)

Tall, slender spikes of star-shaped, bright yellow, fragrant flowers are carried from late spring into early summer above the clumps of slender, grassy, blue-gray leaves.

Crambe cordifolia
HEARTLEAF CRAMBE
☼ ☀ 4-7 ↕ 8ft (2.5m) ↔ 5ft (1.5m)

Tiny, pure white flowers are produced in huge, branching heads above mounds of bold, cabbagelike foliage in early summer. Truly imposing when in full bloom.

Echinops bannaticus 'Taplow Blue'
GLOBE THISTLE
☼ ☀ 3-8 ↕ 4ft (1.2m) ↔ 24in (60cm)

The prickly balls of bright blue flowers in mid- to late summer make this a favorite with both children and butterflies. It has handsome, deeply cut, spiny leaves.

Cortaderia selloana 'Rendatleri'
PINK PAMPAS GRASS
☼ 8-11 ↕ 8ft (2.5m) ↔ 2m (6ft)

A striking ornamental grass with a huge mound of narrow, saw-toothed, evergreen leaves. Tall stems flaunt bold plumes of rosy lilac spikelets during late summer.

Dierama pulcherrimum
WANDFLOWER
☼ 8-9 ↕ 5ft (1.5m) ↔ 4ft (1.2m)

The graceful, arching stems are hung with bell-shaped, dark pink or purple flowers in summer. Its seedheads are attractive too. It is also known as angel's fishing rod.

Eryngium eburneum
SEA HOLLY
☼ 7-10 ↕ 12ft (4m) ↔ 6ft (2m)

This statuesque plant bears tall-stemmed, branching heads of white-green flowers in summer above bold clumps of rapier-like, spine-toothed, evergreen leaves.

Kniphofia 'Prince Igor'
TORCH LILY
☼ ☀ 5-9 ↕6ft (1.8m) ↔36in (90cm)

This outstanding torch lily bears narrow, rich green leaves and many sturdy stems with large, dense pokers of deep orange-red flowers from summer to autumn.

Lavatera 'Kew Rose'
TREE MALLOW
☼ 6-10 ↕↔6ft (2m)

This handsome perennial has branching, woody-based stems bearing gray-green leaves and a succession of pink flowers in summer. It prefers a sheltered spot.

Linaria genistifolia subsp. *dalmatica*
TOADFLAX
☼ 5-8 ↕↔36in (90cm)

Bushy with a creeping rootstock, this toadflax has erect stems crowded with bloomy, blue-green leaves. Spikes of snapdragon-like yellow flowers are borne in summer.

OTHER MEDIUM TO TALL GROWERS FOR SANDY SOIL

Achillea filipendulina, see p.70
Echinops ritro 'Veitch's Blue', see p.73
Eremurus stenophyllus, see p.33
Lilium chalcedonicum
Lilium regale, see p.110
Malva alcea var. *fastigiata*, see p.93
Salvia spp. and cvs.
Verbascum chaixii 'Album', see p.103
Verbena hastata

Perovskia 'Blue Spire'
RUSSIAN SAGE
☼ 4-9 ↕4ft (1.2m) ↔36in (90cm)

This drought-tolerant, woody-based sage has deeply toothed, aromatic, gray-green leaves. Branched spires of tiny, lavender-blue flowers open in summer and autumn.

Romneya coulteri
MATILIJA
☼ 8-11 ↕↔6ft (2m)

A suckering, woody-based perennial or subshrub that forms patches of sea-green, bloomy, leafy stems. During summer, it bears large, yellow-centered flowers.

Salvia cacaliifolia
ORNAMENTAL SAGE
☼ 8-11 ↕4ft (1.2m) ↔36in (90cm)

A robust, branching, tender perennial with triangular leaves and slender sprays of deep blue flowers from midsummer to autumn. It needs a warm, sunny site.

Verbascum 'Gainsborough'
MULLEIN
☼ 5-9 ↕4ft (1.2m) ↔12in (30cm)

Beautiful but short-lived, this mullein has downy, wrinkled leaves in attractive, overwintering rosettes. Branched spires of soft yellow flowers appear in summer.

Low-growing Perennials for Acid Soil

WHILE MOST PERENNIALS thrive in soil that is slightly acid to neutral, a few – including many beloved woodland wildflowers – prefer a site in acid soil that is rich in humus. The perennials below will not grow much above 12in (30cm) tall, making them suitable for lightly shaded woodland edges, rock gardens, or for small peat gardens and beds.

OTHER LOW-GROWING PERENNIALS FOR ACID SOIL

Blechnum penna-marina
Cornus canadensis
Gentiana sino-ornata, see p.55
Phlox stolonifera
Shortia galacifolia
Trillium spp.
Uvularia grandiflora, see p.37
Uvularia perfoliata
Vancouveria hexandra
Viola pedata

Celmisia walkeri
NEW ZEALAND DAISY
9-11 ↕↔ 12in (30cm)

This mat-forming, evergreen perennial has rosettes of leathery, grayish leaves. White, yellow-centered daisies are borne on slender, sticky stems in early summer.

Gentiana 'Kingfisher'
GENTIAN
6-8 ↕ 2in (5cm) ↔ 12in (30cm)

Beautiful trumpet-shaped blue flowers with white and darker blue stripes on the outside open in autumn among the semi-evergreen mats of rosetted, narrow leaves.

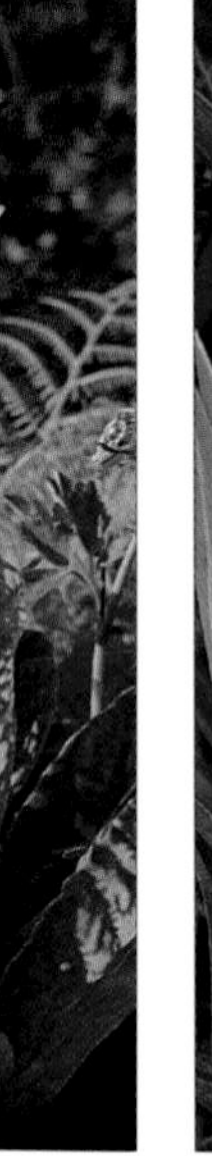

Dodecatheon meadia f. *album*
SHOOTING STAR
4-8 ↕ 16in (40cm) ↔ 10in (25cm)

In spring, loose umbels of nodding white flowers with yellow beaks of stamens are borne on slender stems above a basal rosette of leaves. Prefers humus-rich soil.

Iris 'Arnold Sunrise'
PACIFIC COAST HYBRID IRIS
7-9 ↕ 10in (25cm) ↔ 12in (30cm)

A tough, clump-forming plant producing long, narrow, semievergreen to evergreen leaves. White, yellow-stained flowers are borne in spring. Will tolerate dry soil.

Lithodora diffusa 'Grace Ward'
LITHODORA
6-8 ↕ 6in (15cm) ↔ 36in (90cm)

Deep azure-blue flowers top the prostrate, leafy stems of this dense, carpeting, evergreen perennial or subshrub in late spring and summer. Ideal for rock gardens.

Medium to Tall Perennials for Acid Soil

THE FOLLOWING PERENNIALS all perform best in neutral to acid soil conditions. Many are natives of woodland and mountain sites and require moisture in spring and summer (but not waterlogged soil) in order to thrive. They will grow to around 3ft (1m) or more, and provide superb displays of foliage and flowers for a bed or garden with humus-rich soil.

Blechnum tabulare
BLECHNUM
☼ ◑ 10-11 ↕3ft (1m) ↔4ft (1.2m)

This large, semievergreen to evergreen fern forms a bold clump of leathery sterile fronds. Stiff, fertile fronds crowded with brown spore clusters rise from the center.

Iris ensata 'Variegata'
JAPANESE IRIS
☼ 4-9 ↕36in (90cm) ↔18in (45cm)

This clump-forming iris bears red-purple flowers on upright stems in summer above the clumps of sword-shaped, gray-green, white-striped leaves. Enjoys moist soils.

Lilium auratum
GOLDBAND LILY
☼ ◑ 4-9 ↕5ft (1.5m) ↔12in (30cm)

The tall stems crowded with lance-shaped leaves each bear up to 12 fragrant white flowers, speckled crimson and striped gold, in late summer and early autumn.

Meconopsis chelidoniifolia
MECONOPSIS
◑ 6-9 ↕3ft (1m) ↔24in (60cm)

Elegant yet informal, this plant develops clumps of leafy, slender, semiscandent branching stems. Nodding, saucer-shaped, pale yellow flowers are borne in summer.

Thalictrum rochebruneanum
MEADOW RUE
☼ ◑ 4-7 ↕4ft (1.2m) ↔12in (30cm)

A stately perennial with clumps of large, fernlike leaves and tall stems. Fluffy, lavender-pink flower clusters are borne in summer. Requires moist, humus-rich soil.

OTHER MEDIUM TO TALL PERENNIALS FOR ACID SOIL

Aruncus dioicus, see p.18
Asclepias incarnata
Chelone lyonii
Cimicifuga racemosa
Digitalis purpurea
Dryopteris dilatata
Iris versicolor
Lilium speciosum
Osmunda regalis, see p.61
Smilacina racemosa

Low to Medium Perennials for Alkaline Soil

CONTRARY TO THE popular belief that many of the choicest garden plants demand acid conditions, a wide variety of perennials thrive in, rather than dislike, neutral to alkaline soils. None of the following will grow to more than 3ft (1m) high and are therefore suitable for growing at the front of a border, as well as in raised beds and rock gardens.

Acanthus dioscoridis
BEAR'S-BREECH
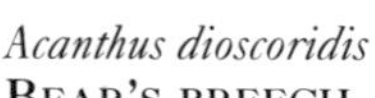
☼ 8-10 ↕16in (40cm) ↔24in (60cm)

A striking perennial forming clumps of lance-shaped, hairy leaves. Dense spikes of rich pink flowers with green bracts are borne during spring and summer.

OTHER LOW TO MEDIUM PERENNIALS FOR ALKALINE SOIL

Anacyclus pyrethrum var. *depressus*
Campanula glomerata
Centranthus ruber, see p.86
Coreopsis grandiflora
Euphorbia rigida
Geranium sanguineum
Gypsophila paniculata
Iris Bearded Hybrids
Platycodon grandiflorus, see p.77
Scabiosa caucasica

Allium cristophii
STAR OF PERSIA
☼ 5-8 ↕24in (60cm) ↔6in (15cm)

Large, globular heads of starry, purple-pink flowers in early summer are followed by decorative seedheads. A spectacular and also very reliable ornamental onion.

Bergenia 'Beethoven'
BERGENIA
☼ ☀ 3-9 ↕18in (45cm) ↔24in (60cm)

This superb German hybrid forms a low clump of bold, leathery leaves. In spring, loose heads of white flowers with reddish calyces are borne above the foliage.

Campanula punctata
BELLFLOWER
☼ ☀ 5-8 ↕↔16in (40cm)

In early summer, this reliable perennial's erect stems are hung with large, tubular, bell-shaped flowers. Blooms are white to dusky pink and heavily spotted within.

Delphinium tatsienense
DELPHINIUM
☼ 7-9 ↕24in (60cm) ↔12in (30cm)

A refreshing change from the tall, spiked hybrids, this delightful species produces slender, branching stems of long-spurred, cornflower blue flowers during summer.

Dianthus 'Mrs. Sinkins'
Old-fashioned Pink
☼ 3-9 ↕16in (40cm) ↔12in (30cm)

Richly fragrant of cloves, this old cottage-garden perennial bears abundant double, fringed, white blossoms in early summer, above evergreen, grayish green leaves.

Francoa sonchifolia
Bridal Wreath
☼ ◐ 7-9 ↕36in (90cm) ↔24in (60cm)

Clumps of evergreen, deeply lobed, hairy leaves are topped in summer by slender pink flower sprays, marked in darker pink. The flowers are excellent for cutting.

Geranium 'Brookside'
Cranesbill
☼ ◐ 5-9 ↕20in (50cm) ↔30in (75cm)

The finely cut leaves of this vigorous plant form a low mound that is covered in summer with showers of saucer-shaped, deep clear blue, white-eyed flowers.

Helleborus x *ericsmithii*
Hellebore
☼ ◐ 6-9 ↕12in (30cm) ↔18in (45cm)

This bold hybrid has attractively marbled, bristle-toothed leaves. It bears large, white or pink-tinted, saucer-shaped flowers in winter. Formerly known as *H.* x *nigristern*.

Lathyrus vernus
Spring Vetchling
☼ ◐ 5-9 ↕12in (30cm) ↔18in (45cm)

The loose racemes of pealike, purplish flowers in spring make this an appealing perennial. Easily grown, its glossy green, deeply divided leaves are attractive too.

Milium effusum 'Aureum'
Golden Wood Millet
◐ 6-9 ↕↔24in (60cm)

Handsome clumps of yellow leaves, fading to yellow-green in summer, are topped by golden seedheads in early summer. It will seed freely and also comes true from seed.

Pulsatilla vulgaris f. *alba*
Pasque Flower
☼ 5-7 ↕↔8in (20cm)

A beautiful white form of a popular plant forming a clump of finely divided, silky-hairy leaves. Silky seedheads follow the white spring flowers.

Viola cornuta
Alba Group
Horned Violet
☼ ◐ 6-9 ↕6in (15cm) ↔12in (30cm)

This violet's long flowering time makes it invaluable. A continuous supply of white flowers tops the mat of toothy, evergreen leaves during spring and summer.

Medium to Tall Perennials for Alkaline Soil

NOT ALL THE PERENNIALS recommended for alkaline soil actually prefer it to acid or neutral soils, but they have proved themselves amenable to these conditions and can be relied upon to do well. The following selection, around 3–10ft (1–3m) high, are some of the most impressive tall perennials suitable for alkaline conditions.

Artemisia lactiflora
WHITE MUGWORT
☼ 4-9 ↕ 5ft (1.5m) ↔ 36in (90cm)

This vigorous plant has dense clumps of erect stems clothed in divided, jaggedly cut leaves. Branched heads of tiny cream flowers open in summer and autumn.

Campanula lactiflora 'Loddon Anna'
GREAT BELLFLOWER
☼ ◐ 3-7 ↕ 5ft (1.5m) ↔ 36in (90cm)

A reliable, easily grown bellflower with conical, branched heads of soft lilac-pink blooms that top the clumps of downy, leafy stems in summer. May need support.

Cortaderia selloana 'Pumila'
PAMPAS GRASS
☼ 8-11 ↕ 5ft (1.5m) ↔ 4ft (1.2m)

This compact cultivar of pampas grass is still large enough to make an impressive specimen for a lawn. Crowded plumes of silvery cream spikelets appear in summer.

Eremurus robustus
DESERT CANDLE, FOXTAIL LILY
☼ 5-8 ↕ 10ft (3m) ↔ 4ft (1.2m)

In summer, magnificent, long-stemmed racemes of star-shaped, pale pink flowers rise above clumps of strap-shaped, blue-green leaves, which wither after flowering.

Euphorbia sikkimensis
SPURGE
☼ ◐ 6-8 ↕ 4ft (1.2m) ↔ 24in (60cm)

The upright stems of this tough, reliable spurge produce narrow, willowlike leaves and yellow flower clusters during summer. Bright pink new shoots appear in spring.

Lavatera 'Barnsley'
TREE MALLOW
☼ 6-9 ↕↔ 6ft (2m)

A succession of white, red-eyed flowers over a long period from spring to autumn and grayish green leaves make this one of the most satisfying of all large perennials.

Oenothera stricta 'Sulphurea'
EVENING PRIMROSE
☼ 5-8 ↕ 36in (90cm) ↔ 6in (15cm)

Over many weeks in summer, this choice perennial bears big, fragrant, pale yellow flowers, which open in the evening on slender, upright stems. It will self-seed.

Phytolacca polyandra
POKEWEED
☼ ☀ 6-9 ↕ 4ft (1.2m) ↔ 24in (60cm)

In autumn, the fleshy stems of this bold perennial turn crimson, the leaves yellow, and dense, erect spikes of striking but poisonous, glistening black fruits appear.

Polygonatum verticillatum
WHORLED SOLOMON'S SEAL
☼ ☀ 4-9 ↕ 36in (90cm) ↔ 12in (30cm)

In early summer, loose clusters of tubular, greenish white flowers, followed by red berries, hang from the slender stems. The leaves are long, slender, and willowlike.

Thalictrum flavum subsp. *glaucum*
YELLOW MEADOW RUE
☀ 4-8 ↕ 5ft (1.5m) ↔ 24in (60cm)

The deeply divided, blue-green, bloomy leaves of this stately plant are invaluable for contrast with greens or purples. Fluffy yellow flowerheads appear in summer.

Veronicastrum virginicum f. *album*
VERONICASTRUM
☼ ☀ 3-8 ↕ 6ft (2m) ↔ 24in (60cm)

Distinctive clumps of slender, stiff, erect stems clothed in whorls of narrow, toothy leaves carry dense, tapering spikes of white flowers from summer to autumn.

OTHER MEDIUM TO TALL PERENNIALS FOR ALKALINE SOIL

Anchusa azurea
Anemone x *hybrida* and cvs.
Buddleia davidii
Campanula latifolia, see p.50
Centaurea macrocephala, see p.18
Echinops ritro, see p.70
Kniphofia spp. and cvs.
Perovskia atriplicifolia
Sidalcea malviflora
Verbascum spp. and cvs.

Perennials for Dry Soil in Sun

WITH THE INCREASING occurrence of water shortages in many regions, perennials that will tolerate dry, sunny conditions are at a premium. Fortunately, a number of plants can survive without rain or watering for long periods. Many of these have long taproots, but densely hairy or waxy leaf-surfaces also help to reduce water loss.

OTHER HERBACEOUS PERENNIALS FOR DRY SOIL IN SUN

Acanthus hirsutus, see p.20
Achillea spp. and cvs.
Cynara cardunculus, see p.130
Echinops ritro 'Veitch's Blue', see p.73
Linum narbonense, see p.21
Pennisetum setaceum
Sedum spp. and cvs.
Sempervivum spp. and cvs.
Stachys byzantina, see p.45
Verbascum chaixii

Anthericum liliago
ST. BERNARD'S LILY
☼ 5-9 ↕36in (90cm) ↔24in (60cm)

This lovely perennial bears tall, elegant racemes of small, lilylike white flowers above its clumps of grassy, grayish green leaves from late spring to early summer.

Asteriscus maritimus
ASTERICUS
☼ 6-9 ↕10in (25cm) ↔36in (90cm)

A woody-based perennial forming a dense carpet or mound studded with daisylike yellow flowerheads during late spring and summer. Its small leaves are roughly-hairy.

Artemisia alba
ARTEMISIA
☼ 5-9 ↕18in (45cm) ↔12in (30cm)

The slender, upright, gray-white stems of this dense, woody-based plant are clothed in aromatic, finely cut, silvery gray foliage, creating an attractive, feathery effect.

Catananche caerulea 'Bicolor'
CUPID'S DART
☼ 4-9 ↕20in (50cm) ↔12in (30cm)

This short-lived perennial forms clumps of grassy leaves. White, purple-centered flowers are produced from midsummer to autumn, each on a single, erect stem.

Crepis incana
PINK DANDELION
☼ 5-7 ↕↔12in (30cm)

During late summer, beautiful, dandelion-like, clear pink flowerheads are borne on slender-branched stems above rosettes of densely hairy, grayish green leaves.

Eryngium x *tripartitum*
ERYNGIUM
☼ 5-8 ↕ 24in (60cm) ↔ 20in (50cm)

Stiff, wiry, many-branched stems produce long-stalked leaves and small heads of violet-blue flowers with prickly gray-blue bracts from summer to autumn.

Papaver orientale 'Perry's White'
ORIENTAL POPPY
☼ 2-7 ↕↔ 36in (90cm)

Deep-rooted clumps of stout, bristly-hairy stems carry large, solitary white flowers with maroon-purple centers in summer over the deeply cut, roughly-hairy leaves.

Phlomis purpurea
PHLOMIS
☼ 7-9 ↕↔ 24in (60cm)

This woody-based perennial or subshrub has woolly shoots and softly-hairy, gray-green leaves. Clusters of pink to purple, two-lipped flowers are borne in summer.

OTHER NATIVE PERENNIALS FOR DRY SOIL IN SUN

Asclepias tuberosa, see p.104
Baptisia australis, see p.92
Echinacea purpurea
Gaillardia aristata
Gaura lindheimeri, see p.108
Liatris punctata
Opuntia humifusa
Rudbeckia maxima
Silphium laciniatum
Yucca filamentosa

Tropaeolum polyphyllum
TROPAEOLUM
☼ 7-9 ↕ 4in (10cm) ↔ 3ft (1m)

Long-spurred, orange- or deep yellow blooms crowd the shoots of this vigorous, trailing plant in summer. Its lobed leaves and fleshy stems are bloomy, blue-green.

Yucca gloriosa
SPANISH DAGGER
☼ 7-10 ↕ 6ft (2m) ↔ 3ft (1m)

Evergreen, sword-shaped, spine-toothed, blue-green leaves crown the short, stout, woody stem. In late summer or autumn, a huge panicle of ivory flowers emerges.

Zauschneria californica subsp. *cana* 'Dublin'
☼ 8-10 ↕ 12in (30cm) ↔ 20in (50cm)

An excellent native perennial for southern gardens with a bushy habit and narrow, downy, gray-green foliage. Tubular red flowers open in late summer and autumn.

Bulbs for Dry Soil in Sun

A GREAT NUMBER OF garden bulbs, including many tulip species, foxtail lilies, and ornamental onions, come from the Mediterranean region and similar warm, sunny, dry areas of the world, including western and central Asia. All of the following bulbs prefer the warmth and brightness of full sun and a site in well-drained soil. The marginally hardy bulbs featured below can be grown outdoors in containers and overwintered in a frost-free place.

Amaryllis belladonna 'Hathor'
BELLADONNA LILY
☼ 8-11 ↕ 24in (60cm) ↔ 4in (10cm)

In time, this plant forms patches of erect, fleshy stems topped by umbels of pure white, trumpet-shaped flowers in autumn. Strap-shaped leaves emerge during spring.

Anomatheca laxa
ANOMATHECA
☼ 8-11 ↕ 8in (20cm) ↔ 3in (8cm)

A charming little plant producing small, irislike leaves and sprays of red flowers in summer. Free-seeding when established, especially in light or sandy soils.

Arum creticum
ARUM
☼ 8-11 ↕ 20in (50cm) ↔ 12in (30cm)

This showy perennial develops clumps of broadly arrow-shaped, rich green leaves in autumn. A white or yellow spathe with a projecting spadix emerges during spring.

Anemone x *fulgens*
SCARLET WINDFLOWER
☼ 6-9 ↕ 10in (25cm) ↔ 6in (15cm)

Brilliant red flowers with darker eyes are borne in spring above deeply cut, bright green leaves. This tuberous perennial is excellent for planting in groups or drifts.

OTHER BULBS FOR DRY SOIL IN SUN

Allium cristophii, see p.26
Allium schubertii
Anemone blanda
Anemone pavonina, see p.52
Calochortus spp.
Colchicum autumnale
Crocus spp. and cvs.
Ipheion uniflorum
Iris bucharica
Ixiolirion tataricum
Lilium candidum
Lilium regale, see p.110
Lilium x *testaceum*
Oxalis adenophylla, see p.55
Pancratium illyricum, see p.41
Sternbergia lutea
Triteleia laxa
Tulipa kaufmanniana

Dracunculus vulgaris
DRAGON ARUM
☼ 5-11 ↕ 36in (90cm) ↔ 24in (60cm)

The darkly mottled stems of this strange and striking perennial produce deeply divided, long-stalked leaves and velvety, deep maroon-purple flowers in summer.

Eremurus stenophyllus
FOXTAIL LILY
☼ 5-9 ↕3ft (1m) ↔24in (60cm)

This perennial has a divided, fleshy crown that produces a cluster of strap-shaped grayish leaves. Tall spires of starry yellow, pink, or white flowers appear in summer.

Gladiolus communis subsp. *byzantinus*
HARDY GLADIOLUS
☼ 6-10 ↕3ft (1m) ↔10in (25cm)

Reliable and also easy to grow, this robust perennial forms clumps of narrow, sword-like leaves that sport bold spikes of vivid magenta flowers during summer.

Hermodactylus tuberosus
WIDOW IRIS
☼ 5-8 ↕12in (30cm) ↔4in (10cm)

This curious iris relative has a somber charm. In spring, green or greenish yellow flowers join the narrow, grassy leaves. The outer petals have blackish brown tips.

Scilla peruviana
CUBAN LILY
☼ 8-11 ↕12in (30cm) ↔6in (15cm)

The clumps of broad, strap-shaped, fleshy green leaves are topped during late spring by striking, large, conical heads of small, star-shaped, blue to blue-violet flowers.

Triteleia hyacinthina
WILD HYACINTH
☼ 6-11 ↕28in (70cm) ↔2in (5cm)

Like a white-flowered ornamental onion without the smell, this very attractive and reliable bulb bears umbels of star-shaped flowers on slender stems in early summer.

Tulipa clusiana
LADY TULIP
☼ 4-8 ↕12in (30cm) ↔4in (10cm)

A beautiful tulip producing narrow grayish leaves and white spring flowers with dark crimson eyes. Crimson backs to the outer petals give blooms a striped appearance.

Tulipa tarda
TULIP
☼ 4-8 ↕6in (15cm) ↔4in (10cm)

This reliable and lovely small tulip species produces a rosette of glossy, narrow leaves and bears star-shaped yellow flowers with white tips above the foliage during spring.

Perennials for Dry Soil in Shade

Dry, shady sites are one of the most difficult garden situations to deal with successfully. One easy solution is to plant these areas with the perennials listed here. Avoid planting in the soil under shallow-rooted trees, like maples; simply mulch these sites instead. Under deep-rooted trees, such as oaks, dig "planting pockets" between the roots.

Other Perennial Groundcovers for Dry Soil in Shade

Convallaria majalis
Epimedium spp. and cvs.
Helleborus x *hybridus*, see p.84
Lamium maculatum 'Beacon Silver', see p.85
Liriope muscari, see p.65
Ophiopogon japonicus
Pachysandra terminalis
Vinca major
Waldsteinia ternata

Buglossoides purpurocaerulea
Purple Gromwell
☼ ◐ 6-8 ↕ 24in (60cm) ↔ 36in (90cm)

This handsome, low-growing perennial sends out long shoots that root at the tips. From late spring to summer, erect stems bear purple flowers that turn deep blue.

Epimedium perralderianum
Epimedium
◐ ● 5-8 ↕ 12in (30cm) ↔ 24in (60cm)

A semievergreen or evergreen perennial with bright yellow spring flowers. The glossy, dark green leaves, each with three leaflets, are bronze-colored when young.

Claytonia sibirica
Siberian Purslane
◐ ● 5-9 ↕ 8in (20cm) ↔ 6in (15cm)

Short-lived but free-seeding, this plant develops tufts of fleshy green leaves and freely bears loose heads of small pink or white flowers from late spring to summer.

Euphorbia amygdaloides var. *robbiae*
Wood Spurge
◐ ● 6-8 ↕ 30in (75cm) ↔ 24in (60cm)

A vigorous, creeping perennial with erect stems bearing leathery, dark green leaves. Crowded racemes of greenish yellow flowers appear in spring and early summer.

Other Perennials for Dry Soil in Shade

Cyclamen hederifolium, see p.96
Dicentra eximia
Dryopteris filix-mas
Geranium macrorrhizum, see p.83
Helleborus foetidus
Hyacinthoides non-scripta
Polygonatum odoratum
Polypodium vulgare
Polystichum acrostichoides
Pulmonaria saccharata

Geranium phaeum 'Album'
HARDY GERANIUM
☼ ◐ 5-8 ↕32in (80cm) ↔18in (45cm)

A lovely geranium bearing showers of pendent white, yellow-beaked flowers above semievergreen clumps of shallowly lobed, soft green leaves in mid spring.

Iris foetidissima var. *citrina*
STINKING IRIS
◐ ● 6-9 ↕30in (75cm) ↔24in (60cm)

A useful and adaptable evergreen with clumps of strong-smelling, strap-shaped, shiny leaves and yellow summer flowers. It bears pods of orange seeds in autumn.

Lamium galeobdolon 'Hermann's Pride'
◐ ● 4-9 ↕24in (60cm) ↔4ft (1.2m)

A tough groundcover producing spreading mounds of handsome, silver-marbled leaves. It produces clusters of two-lipped yellow flowers in the leaf axils in summer.

Saxifraga stolonifera
STRAWBERRY GERANIUM
◐ ● 3-9 ↕12in (30cm) ↔8in (20cm)

Red runners, forming new plantlets at their tips, grow from the rosettes of long-stalked, pale-veined leaves. Erect stems bear tiny white flowers in summer.

Symphytum 'Hidcote Pink'
COMFREY
☼ ◐ 5-9 ↕↔18in (45cm)

An excellent, creeping perennial groundcover forming low patches of erect, leafy stems. Pendent clusters of funnel-shaped, pink and white flowers emerge in spring.

Tolmiea menziesii
PIGGY-BACK PLANT
◐ ● 6-9 ↕↔24in (60cm)

A creeping perennial with loose clumps of hairy leaves that bear new plants at their bases. In spring and summer, airy panicles of tiny, brownish green flowers appear.

Trachystemon orientalis
TRACHYSTEMON
☼ ◐ 5-9 ↕12in (30cm) ↔indefinite

A creeping plant eventually forming large, dense patches of long-stalked, roughly-hairy leaves. The bristly stems bear blue flowers with "beaks" of stamens in spring.

Perennials for Moist Soil in Shade

Some of the most exquisite perennials are native to deciduous woodlands where they receive protection from the harsh summer sun. These woodland plants are obvious choices for a wildflower garden, but are also ideal for beds on the shady side of the house, under trees, and other cool sites where moisture is guaranteed during the growing season.

Other Perennials for Moist Soil in Shade

- *Anemonella thalictroides*
- *Cimicifuga* spp. and cvs.
- *Dicentra eximia* and cvs.
- *Hepatica* spp. and cvs.
- *Jeffersonia diphylla*
- *Mertensia virginica*
- *Polygonatum humile*
- *Tricyrtis hirta* and cvs.
- *Trillium grandiflorum*
- *Vancouveria hexandra*

Actaea rubra
Red Baneberry
☼ 4-8 ↕18in (45cm) ↔12in (30cm)

A poisonous plant but well worth growing for its clump of deeply divided leaves and dense, terminal clusters of shining red berries borne in late summer and autumn.

Anemonopsis macrophylla
False Anemone
☼ 5-8 PH ↕30in (75cm) ↔18in (45cm)

This handsome woodland plant produces a clump of ferny leaves and bears delicate sprays of cup-shaped, nodding, waxy, lilac and violet flowers during late summer.

Convallaria majalis var. *rosea*
Lily-of-the-Valley
☼ ☀ 4-9 ↕8in (20cm) ↔12in (30cm)

This very pretty variant of a much-loved perennial forms a carpet of paired leaves. It bears loose racemes of nodding, mauve-pink, bell-shaped flowers during spring.

Corydalis flexuosa
Blue False Bleeding Heart
☼ 5-8 ↕↔12in (30cm)

During spring and early summer, showers of blue flowers are carried above the ferny, blue-green foliage. The leaves emerge in autumn and die down in summer.

Dactylorhiza foliosa
Maderian Orchid
☼ 7-8 ↕24in (60cm) ↔6in (15cm)

In time, this terrestrial orchid develops a clump of stout, lush, leafy stems. These sport bold, dense spikes of bright purple flowers in late spring or early summer.

Deinanthe caerulea
Deinanthe
☼ 5-9 ↕↔12in (30cm)

The attractive, crinkly green leaves of this choice, creeping perennial will eventually form a clump. Loose panicles of nodding, fleshy blue flowers open during summer.

Glaucidium palmatum
GLAUCIDIUM

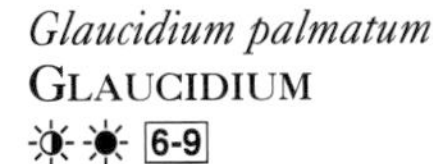

☼ ☀ 6-9 ↕↔ 18in (45cm)

This lovely woodlander produces a clump of large, attractively lobed and toothed leaves. In late spring and early summer, it bears poppylike mauve or lilac flowers.

Trillium cernuum
NODDING TRILLIUM

☼ ☀ 5-9 PH ↕ 20in (50cm) ↔ 12in (30cm)

Impressive when planted in groups, this charming perennial has clumps of broad, wavy-edged leaves and small, nodding, white to pale pink or red flowers in spring.

Trillium sessile
TOADSHADE

☼ ☀ 5-9 PH ↕↔ 12in (30cm)

This native woodland plant has broad, often beautifully marbled, three-parted leaves. The stemless, erect, red or maroon flowers are produced during spring.

Hacquetia epipactis
HACQUETIA

☼ 5-7 ↕ 6in (15cm) ↔ 12in (30cm)

One of the earliest woodlanders to appear in spring, bearing curious, collared, yellow-green flowerheads followed by emerald-green leaves. Both useful and reliable.

Sanguinaria canadensis 'Plena'
DOUBLE BLOODROOT

☼ ☀ 3-9 ↕ 6in (15cm) ↔ 12in (30cm)

Lovely white blooms open in early spring as leaves appear. The lobed, gray-green leaves are loosely rolled around the stem upon emergence. Dies down by summer.

Uvularia grandiflora
GREAT MERRYBELLS

☼ ☀ 3-9 ↕ 30in (75cm) ↔ 12in (30cm)

This favorite native woodland plant forms a clump of erect, slender, leafy shoots with nodding tips. During spring, the shoots carry pendent, bell-shaped yellow flowers.

Bulbs for Moist Soil in Shade

MANY OF THE MOST POPULAR and best-loved bulbs thrive in the cool, moist soils and partial shade of deciduous woodlands. There they receive sun in early spring and shade in summer when trees are leafy. Most are easy to grow and will thrive in a shady site with minimum care. Some will form large colonies where space and conditions permit.

Allium moly
LILY LEEK
☼ ☀ 4-8 ↕10in (25cm) ↔4in (10cm)

This bulb soon forms substantial clumps of broad, strap-shaped gray leaves. It bears umbels of star-shaped yellow flowers in early summer. Also ideal for a site in sun.

Arisaema triphyllum
JACK-IN-THE-PULPIT
☼ ☀ 3-9 ↕24in (60cm) ↔6in (15cm)

A woodland plant with long-stalked green leaves divided into threes and hooded green, sometimes dark-striped, flowers in spring. Red berries are borne in autumn.

Cardiocrinum giganteum var. *yunnanense*
GIANT LILY
☀ 7-10 ↕8ft (2.5m) ↔18in (45cm)

Tall, erect, dark stems have heart-shaped leaves and bear long heads of pendent, fragrant, creamy white flowers in summer. The parent plant dies after flowering.

Arisaema sikokianum
JACK-IN-THE-PULPIT
☀ 5-8 ↕16in (40cm) ↔6in (15cm)

A striking perennial with often beautifully marked leaves divided into threes. The dark flowers borne in spring have striped spathes and a contrasting white spadix.

Brimeura amethystina
BRIMEURA
☼ ☀ 5-8 ↕8in (20cm) ↔3in (8cm)

Resembling a small, slender hyacinth, this bulb bears one-sided racemes of tubular, bright blue flowers in late spring or early summer. Will spread freely in a good site.

Erythronium 'Pagoda'
TROUT LILY
☀ 5-8 ↕14in (35cm) ↔4in (10cm)

In spring, dark stems bear pendent yellow flowers with upswept petals above lush rosettes of mottled green leaves. This is a vigorous bulb that self-seeds when happy.

OTHER BULBS FOR MOIST SOIL IN SHADE

Anemone blanda
Anemone nemorosa
Arisaema ringens
Arisarum proboscideum
Arum italicum 'Marmoratum', see p.135
Begonia grandis
Camassia leichtlinii, see p.52
Corydalis flexuosa 'China Blue', see p.65
Corydalis solida
Cyclamen coum
Eranthis hyemalis, see p.98
Galanthus ikariae
Hyacinthoides hispanica, see p.53
Hyacinthoides non-scripta
Ipheion uniflorum
Leucojum vernum
Ornithogalum nutans
Scilla spp. and cvs.

Erythronium revolutum
TROUT LILY
☀ 5-8 ↕12in (30cm) ↔4in (10cm)

Rosettes of beautifully mottled leaves are topped by elegant pink, yellow-centered flowers in spring. This is one of the best trout lilies for cultivation. May seed freely.

Leucojum aestivum 'Gravetye Giant'
SUMMER SNOWFLAKE
☼ ☀ 4-9 ↕36in (90cm) ↔4in (10cm)

This robust and easily grown bulb quickly forms erect clumps of green leaves. The pretty umbels of nodding white, green-tipped flowers are produced in late spring.

Galanthus elwesii
GIANT SNOWDROP
☀ 3-9 ↕9in (22cm) ↔3in (8cm)

Easy to grow and reliable, this variable bulb usually has narrow, gray-green leaves and white flowers in late winter with inner segments marked green at both ends.

Galanthus plicatus
SNOWDROP
☀ 3-9 ↕8in (20cm) ↔3in (8cm)

This vigorous snowdrop has narrow, dark green leaves with folded-under edges. Its late winter flowers have green-tipped inner segments. In time it forms colonies.

Narcissus pseudonarcissus
DAFFODIL
☼ ☀ 5-8 ↕14in (35cm) ↔4in (10cm)

A charming, spring-flowering woodland species bearing pale yellow flowers with deep yellow trumpets that are flared at the mouths. Excellent for naturalizing.

Perennials for Warm, Sheltered Sites

For those fortunate enough to garden in mild regions, there are many exciting, often exotic-looking, perennials that are easy to grow. Some of these will also survive in colder areas if they are given a warm, sheltered site. Gardeners in northern regions can enjoy these perennials by growing them in containers and moving them indoors for winter.

Erythrina crista-galli
Cockspur Coral-tree
☼ 9-11 ↕ 6ft (2m) ↔ 4ft (1.2m)

Herbaceous or woody-based in cold areas, this plant forms a shrub or small tree in frost-free regions. In late summer, strong, thorny stems bear red pea-shaped flowers.

Begonia sutherlandii
Begonia
☼ 8-10 ↕↔ 18in (45cm)

In summer, drooping clusters of orange, red-stalked flowers are borne freely above the low mounds of fleshy red stems and pointed, toothed leaves.

Bletilla striata 'Albostriata'
Bletilla
☼ ◐ 6-9 ↕↔ 24in (60cm)

A beautiful terrestrial orchid eventually forming patches of strongly veined, white-margined, bamboolike leaves. Magenta flowers open in spring and early summer.

Crinum x *powellii*
Crinum
☼ 7-10 ↕ 4ft (1.2m) ↔ 24in (60cm)

In late summer and autumn, stout, fleshy stems carry loose umbels of fragrant, lily-like pink blooms above the bold clumps of long, arching, strap-shaped leaves.

Eucomis comosa
Pineapple Flower
☼ 8-10 ↕ 24in (60cm) ↔ 12in (30cm)

Dense racemes of greenish white flowers with leafy tufts at the top rise on fleshy stems in late summer above bold rosettes of strap-shaped, shiny green leaves.

Fascicularia pitcairniifolia
FASCICULARIA
☼ 10-11 ↕↔ 24in (60cm)

A striking relative of the pineapple with narrow, spine-toothed, evergreen leaves in bold rosettes. In summer, the inner leaves turn red when powdery blue flowers open.

OTHER PERENNIALS FOR WARM, SHELTERED SITES

Convolvulus sabatinus, see p.58
Cortaderia selloana 'Pumila', see p.28
Eucomis bicolor, see p.64
Euphorbia characias
Fuschia magellanica
Gladiolus communis
Kniphofia spp. and cvs.
Lavandula stoechas, see p.73
Lavatera cachemiriana
Lespedeza juncea

Hedychium gardnerianum
KAHILI GINGER
☼ 8-11 ↕ 6ft (2m) ↔ 3ft (1m)

This vigorous perennial forms a clump of erect, leafy stems. These bear large heads of fragrant, pale yellow flowers with long, red stamens during late summer.

Lobelia laxiflora var. *angustifolia*
LOBELIA
☼ 8-10 ↕ 24in (60cm) ↔ 3ft (1m)

The erect, woody-based stems of this fast-spreading lobelia bear narrow, willowlike leaves and lax, tubular, red-and-yellow flowers in late spring and early summer.

Melianthus major
HONEY BUSH
☼ 9-11 ↕ 6ft (2m) ↔ 3ft (1m)

A spectacular foliage plant with a clump of large, lush, sharply toothed and deeply divided, bluish gray leaves. Spikes of brownish red flowers emerge in summer.

Pancratium illyricum
SEA LILY
☼ 8-11 ↕↔ 16in (40cm)

In late summer, this bulbous perennial produces umbels of fragrant, star-shaped white flowers on erect stems above bold clumps of strap-shaped, gray-green leaves.

Puya alpestris
PUYA
☼ 10-11 ↕ 5ft (1.5m) ↔ 4½ft (1.4m)

After several years, the evergreen rosette of narrow, spine-toothed leaves produces an erect stem topped by a striking, dense spike of waxy, blue-green summer blooms.

OTHER TENDER PERENNIALS FOR WARM, SHELTERED SITES

Abutilon x *hybridum*
Agapanthus spp. and cvs.
Beschorneria yuccoides
Brugmansia spp. and cvs.
Fascicularia bicolor
Helichrysum petiolare
Geranium maderense
Nierembergia 'Mount Blanc'
Pelargonium spp. and cvs.
Plectranthus argentatus

Senecio pulcher
SENECIO
☼ 8-11 ↕ 24in (60cm) ↔ 20in (50cm)

The basal clumps of semievergreen, long, scalloped leaves are woolly when young. Attractive, large, carmine-purple, yellow-centered flowerheads emerge in summer.

SPECIFIC USES

WHETHER YOU WANT plants to fill a difficult site, to provide cut flowers or foliage, or to attract bees and butterflies to your garden, perennials have the variety and versatility to answer your needs. A good choice of plants is usually available to solve even the most specific garden problems.

△ LOVED BY BUTTERFLIES *The flowers of perennials like* Inula hookeri *attract bees, butterflies, and other welcome insects.*

Houttuynia cordata 'Chameleon' for water gardens

The plants in this section have been selected to help you find the right perennials for specific garden features (such as rock or water gardens), conditions (including dry, exposed, or waterlogged sites), and garden problems (like pollution or pests). When choosing plants for a particular garden feature or site, the most suitable are usually those that grow in similar situations in the wild. Water and bog gardens, for instance, require plants that are naturally tolerant of wet soils. At the other extreme, rock gardens are suited to perennials that thrive, if not depend, on sharp drainage. Similarly, coastal gardens in exposed sites require robust plants like sea holly (*Eryngium*) that are adapted to the harsh conditions. Toughness and persistence are also needed by perennials naturalized in grass, along hedges, or other wild areas, where the ability to withstand competition is vital for survival.

PROBLEM SOLVERS

Perennials offer more than just a wide range of options for specific sites; they can also help us address some of the problems that often plague our gardens. Pests, such as slugs, deer, and rabbits, may be thwarted by a surprising number of unpalatable plants. The garden can also be stocked with many low-allergen (mostly insect-pollinated) perennials, useful for gardeners who suffer from allergies that are aggravated or induced by plants.

DECORATIVE VALUE

The wide-ranging ornamental uses of perennials are not always fully appreciated. Many are excellent for containers on shady or sunny patios or paved areas, or for specimen plants. Others produce foliage and flowers good for cutting, extending their garden value into the home. During quiet periods in the garden, dried seedheads can provide the material for arrangements.

△ NATURAL EFFECT *Many perennials, especially bulbs like these fritillarias, are excellent for naturalizing in grassy sites.*

◁ ROCK GARDEN *Perennials from well-drained, rocky habitats in the wild will thrive in a rock garden or wall.*

▷ WATERSIDE *A pond planted with lush marginal and aquatic perennials makes a bold feature and a good wildlife habitat.*

Perennial Groundcovers for Sun

IN ADDITION TO BEING ORNAMENTAL, groundcovers perform one of the most useful and valuable jobs in the garden by clothing bare ground. The best perennials for this purpose are usually fast-growing. Given a sunny site, the following will repay you by providing a superb display of foliage and flowers. For faster results, plant these perennials in groups.

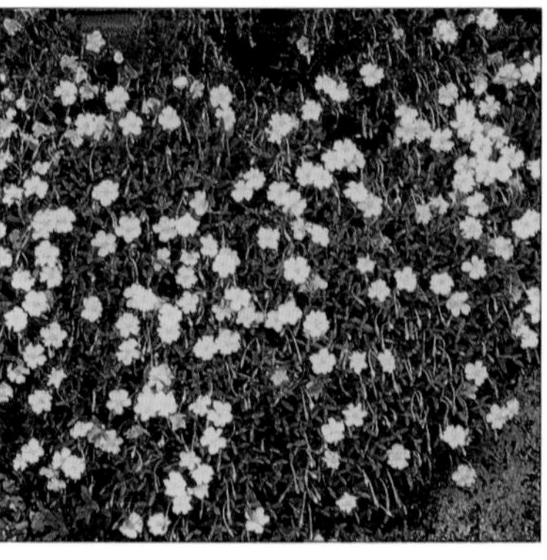

Helianthemum lunulatum
ROCKROSE, SUNROSE
☼ 6-9 ↕ 6in (15cm) ↔ 12in (30cm)

A carpeting, woody-based perennial with grayish green, evergreen leaves. Clusters of yellow flowers with orange-yellow stamens open in late spring and summer.

OTHER EVERGREEN PERENNIAL GROUNDCOVERS FOR SUN

Arabis caucasica
Aubrieta deltoidea
Dianthus spp. and cvs.
Festuca glauca 'Elijah Blue'
Globularia cordifolia
Iberis sempervirens
Liriope muscari, see p.65
Potentilla neumanniana
Sasa veitchii, see p.135
Sedum kamtschaticum

Ceratostigma plumbaginoides
PLUMBAGO LEADWORT
☼ 5-9 ↕ 12in (30cm) ↔ 18in (45cm)

This vigorous perennial develops a dense patch of bright green leaves that turn red-orange in autumn. The clusters of rich blue flowers emerge during late summer.

Diascia 'Salmon Supreme'
DIASCIA
☼ 7-9 ↕ 6in (15cm) ↔ 20in (50cm)

This free-flowering plant bears abundant slender racemes of pale flowers during summer and autumn above mats of small, heart-shaped, semievergreen leaves.

Geranium 'Ann Folkard'
CRANESBILL
☼ ◐ 5-8 ↕ 24in (60cm) ↔ 5ft (1.5m)

Few cranesbills will flower or scramble as freely as this one, which has black-eyed magenta flowers in summer and autumn above deeply lobed, yellow-green leaves.

Persicaria vacciniifolia
PERSICARIA
☼ ◐ 4-8 ↕ 6in (15cm) ↔ 12in (30cm)

This fast-creeping plant forms a carpet of small, glossy green leaves that color richly in autumn. Erect, deep pink flower spikes open from late summer into autumn.

OTHER HERBACEOUS PERENNIAL GROUNDCOVERS FOR SUN

Antennaria dioica
Artemisia stelleriana
Campanula carpatica
Cerastium tomentosum, see p.130
Geranium sanguineum var. *striatum*
Oenothera tetragona
Potentilla aurea
Potentilla tridentata
Saponaria ocymoides
Thymus serpyllum

Phyla nodiflora
CAPEWEED, MATGRASS
☼ 10-11 ↕2in (5cm) ↔ indefinite

Sometimes sold as *Lippia*, this perennial soon forms carpets of slender stems and small leaves. Long-stalked clusters of tiny flowers are borne in summer and autumn.

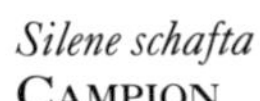

Silene schafta
CAMPION
☼ ☼ 4-8 ↕10in (25cm) ↔ 12in (30cm)

Slender stems and semievergreen, bright green leaves form a low mound, good for edging. Long-tubed, red-pink flowers are borne freely from summer to autumn.

Rhodanthemum hosmariense
RHODANTHEMUM
☼ 8-10 ↕↔ 12in (30cm)

A low and spreading, woody-based plant with dense, finely divided, silvery downy leaves. The large daisy flowers are borne freely from early spring to autumn.

Sedum spurium 'Schorbuser Blut'
STONECROP
☼ 3-8 ↕4in (10cm) ↔ 24in (60cm)

Popular as a vigorous carpeter, this stonecrop has glossy, evergreen leaves that are purple-tinted when mature. Star-shaped, deep pink flowers open in late summer.

Stachys byzantina
LAMB'S EARS
☼ 4-8 ↕15in (38cm) ↔ 24in (60cm)

A very effective groundcover producing rosettes of white-woolly, semievergreen leaves. White-woolly, pink-purple flower spikes rise above the foliage in summer.

Perennial Groundcovers for Shade

SHADY AREAS CAN SUPPORT a wealth of plants as long as the soil remains sufficiently moist. Shade-loving perennials with creeping or otherwise spreading and low-growing habits are useful and attractive when used as groundcovers under shrubs or trees. Many are also evergreen, and will brighten shady spots with their year-round carpets of foliage.

Ajuga reptans 'Jungle Beauty'
BUGLEWEED

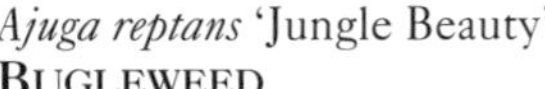

3-9 ↕ 6in (15cm) ↔ 3ft (1m)

Grown here with *Lysimachia nummularia* 'Aurea', this semievergreen, far-creeping carpeter has shiny, bronze-green leaves and rich blue flower spikes in late spring.

OTHER EVERGREEN PERENNIAL GROUNDCOVERS FOR SHADE

- *Asarum europaeum*, see p.114
- *Blechnum penna-marina*
- *Euphorbia amygdaloides* var. *robbiae*, see p.34
- *Helleborus orientalis*
- *Heuchera americana* and cvs.
- *Liriope* spp. and cvs.
- *Mitchella repens*
- *Pachysandra terminalis* 'Variegata'
- *Saxifraga stolonifera*, see p.35

Chrysogonum virginianum
GREEN-AND-GOLD, GOLDEN STAR

5-8 ↕ 10in (25cm) ↔ 24in (60cm)

This fast-growing woodland plant forms dense carpets of small, semievergreen leaves. Bright and cheerful yellow flowers are produced during spring and summer.

Cyclamen repandum subsp. *peloponnesiacum*

7-9 ↕ 4in (10cm) ↔ 6in (15cm)

A tuberous perennial that forms patches of heart-shaped, scalloped, silver-speckled leaves. Fragrant, pale pink flowers with darker pink mouths are borne in spring.

Duchesnea indica
MOCK STRAWBERRY

4-9 ↕ 4in (10cm) ↔ 4ft (1.2m)

The dense, fast-growing carpet of semi-evergreen, strawberrylike leaves is dotted with yellow flowers in summer. The fruits resemble strawberries but are unpalatable.

Epimedium pinnatum subsp. *colchicum*
EPIMEDIUM

4-10 ↕↔ 16in (40cm)

One of the most reliable epimediums, this forms clumps of slightly spiny-margined, semievergreen leaves topped in spring by loose spires of small yellow flowers.

Geranium macrorrhizum 'Czakor'
WILD CRANESBILL

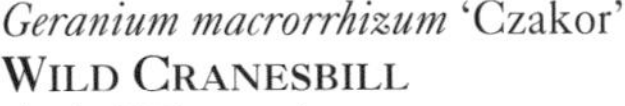

3-8 ↕12in (30cm) ↔24in (60cm)

A first-rate carpeter with lobed, aromatic, semievergreen leaves that become purple-tinted in autumn. It bears profuse, small magenta flowers during early summer.

Tiarella cordifolia
ALLEGHENY FOAMFLOWER

3-8 ↕10in (25cm) ↔12in (30cm)

A reliable old favorite especially pretty in late spring when foamy spires of white flowers rise above the foliage. The leaves are often tinted bronze-red in autumn.

OTHER HERBACEOUS PERENNIAL GROUNDCOVERS FOR SHADE

Aegopodium podagraria 'Variegatum'
Asarum canadense
Convallaria majalis 'Fortin's Giant'
Cyclamen hederifolium, see p.96
Galium odoratum
Hosta spp. and cvs.
Maianthemum bifolium
Pachysandra procumbens
Pulmonaria angustifolia
Vancouveria hexandra

Lamium galeobdolon 'Florentinum'
YELLOW ARCHANGEL

4-9 ↕24in (60cm) ↔6ft (2m)

One of the most striking, but invasive, groundcovers. It produces semievergreen, silver-zoned leaves and bears spires of two-lipped yellow flowers in summer.

Gymnocarpium dryopteris
OAK FERN

2-5 PH ↕8in (20cm) ↔12in (30cm)

Delicate looking but hardy, this little fern forms a low patch of triangular, prettily divided fronds on slender, wiry stems. It requires cool, moist conditions to thrive.

Meehania urticifolia
MEEHAN'S MINT

6-9 ↕12in (30cm) ↔6ft (2m)

In time, this vigorous perennial forms clumps of heart-shaped leaves. One-sided spikes of two-lipped, deep violet flowers are borne in late spring and early summer.

Vinca minor 'Gertrude Jekyll'
COMMON PERIWINKLE

4-9 ↕6in (15cm) ↔indefinite

Technically a creeping shrub, but a good groundcover for use with perennials. The white flowers in spring and early summer contrast with the dark green leaves.

Perennial Herbs for Borders

PERENNIALS VALUED FOR their culinary uses or medicinal attributes are frequently cultivated in separate herb gardens or combined with vegetables in kitchen gardens. This certainly makes it much more convenient for picking or harvesting, but does not always make the best use of these plants' varied growth habits, or their often ornamental foliage and flowers. In fact, herbs can be grown just as easily, and more effectively, with other perennials in beds and borders.

Achillea ptarmica 'Boule de Neige'
SNEEZEWORT
☼ 2-9 ↕24in (60cm) ↔18in (45cm)

The clumps of erect stems and narrow, toothed, dark green leaves are smothered during summer with small, double white flowerheads. All parts have medicinal uses.

Agastache foeniculum
ANISE HYSSOP
☼ 6-9 ↕36in (90cm) ↔18in (45cm)

Spikes of blue flowers with violet bracts top the four-angled stems during summer. The softly-downy, anise-scented leaves are used as a fragrant tea and in potpourri.

Allium schoenoprasum 'Forescate'
CHIVES
☼ 3-9 ↕24in (60cm) ↔5in (12.5cm)

An attractive, vigorous form of a kitchen-garden favorite with clumps of hollow, edible leaves. The dense heads of bright purplish pink flowers open in summer.

Althaea officinalis
MARSH MALLOW
☼ ☀ 3-9 ↕6ft (2m) ↔5ft (1.5m)

Loose clumps of erect, downy stems bear velvety, grayish, three-lobed leaves and pink late-summer flowers. Its root sugars were once used to make marshmallows.

Aristolochia clematitis
BIRTHWORT
☼ ☀ 5-9 ↕36in (90cm) ↔24in (60cm)

Curious, slender-tubed yellow flowers emerge from the axils of the heart-shaped leaves in summer. The creeping rootstock forms spreading clumps of erect stems.

OTHER PERENNIAL HERBS FOR BORDERS

Armoracia rusticana 'Variegata', see p.126
Cichorium intybus 'Roseum', see p.76
Foeniculum vulgare 'Purpureum', see p.119
Lavandula angustifolia
Mentha suaveolens 'Variegata'
Monarda fistulosa
Origanum vulgare 'Gold Tip'
Pulmonaria officinalis
Ruta graveolens
Salvia officinalis 'Icterina', see p.121
Saponaria officinalis 'Rosea Plena'
Scutellaria baicalensis
Symphytum peregrinum 'Rubrum'
Tanacetum balsamita subsp. *balsamitoides*
Tanacetum parthenium

Melissa officinalis 'Aurea'
LEMON BALM
☼ 4-9 ↕24in (60cm) ↔18in (45cm)

The hairy green, yellow-splashed leaves of this vigorous, bushy plant are lemon-scented when bruised. Tiny flowers, loved by bees, are produced during summer.

Myrrhis odorata
SWEET CICELY
☼ ☀ 3-7 ↕36in (90cm) ↔5ft (1.5m)

All parts of this plant are anise-scented. It produces bold clumps of hollow stems, ferny leaves, and flattened heads of white summer flowers followed by brown fruits.

Rumex scutatus 'Silver Shield'
FRENCH SORREL
☼ 4-8 ↕20in (50cm) ↔12in (30cm)

This small, woody-based perennial has prostrate and upright stems with broadly arrow-shaped, silver-green-topped leaves. Spires of green flowers open in summer.

Levisticum officinale
LOVAGE
☼ 5-8 ↕6ft (2m) ↔3ft (1m)

Much-divided, dark green leaves clothe the erect clumps of smooth, hollow stems. During summer, the stems are topped by umbels of pretty, greenish yellow flowers.

Origanum vulgare 'Aureum'
GOLDEN WILD MARJORAM
☼ 5-9 ↕18in (45cm) ↔12in (30cm)

Spreading clumps of four-angled stems are crowded with rounded, aromatic golden leaves. Plants bear dense clusters of pink flowers from summer to autumn.

Salvia officinalis 'Tricolor'
COMMON SAGE
☼ 5-8 ↕32in (80cm) ↔3ft (1m)

A woody-based semievergreen plant or bushy subshrub bearing aromatic, woolly, gray-green leaves with cream, purple, and pink zones. It has blue flowers in summer.

Perennials for Wild Margins and along Hedges

MANY OF THE LOVELIEST WILDFLOWERS are frequently found thriving beside roads or at the bases of hedges. These bold perennials, which can tolerate competition from grasses, shrubs, and other plants, will make fine additions to gardens in the right site. Use them along uncultivated garden edges or to add a colorful display to a hedge base.

Anemone x *hybrida* 'Königin Charlotte'
JAPANESE ANEMONE
5-8 ↕5ft (1.5m) ↔indefinite

A vigorous perennial forming colonies of branched stems with handsome, downy, gray-green leaves. Big, semidouble pink flowers open in late summer and autumn.

Carex pendula
DROOPING SEDGE
5-9 ↕4ft (1.2m) ↔5ft (1.5m)

Arching, three-cornered stems and dark green leaves form large clumps topped in late spring and summer by long, pendent green flower spikes. Prefers moist shade.

Heliopsis helianthoides subsp. *scabra* 'Sommersonne'
3-9 ↕36in (90cm) ↔24in (60cm)

The bold clumps of leafy, branched stems carry large, single to semidouble, golden yellow daisy flowers with brown-yellow centers during late summer and autumn.

Campanula latifolia
GREAT BELLFLOWER
3-7 ↕5ft (1.5m) ↔24in (60cm)

In summer, the stout clumps of erect leafy stems produce large, bell-shaped, pale to deep violet or white flowers from the axils of the uppermost leaves.

Helianthus x *multiflorus*
PERENNIAL SUNFLOWER
4-8 ↕6ft (2m) ↔36in (90cm)

Dark green leaves clothe the tall clumps of branching stems, which produce yellow, dark-centered daisy flowers during late summer and autumn. Prefers a moist site.

Lathyrus latifolius
PERENNIAL PEA
5-9 ↕↔6ft (2m)

This vigorous, herbaceous climbing plant produces long-stalked racemes of pink or purple, pea-shaped flowers from summer to autumn on scrambling, winged stems.

OTHER LOW-GROWING PERENNIALS FOR WILD AREAS

Convallaria majalis
Epimedium spp. and cvs.
Euphorbia amygdaloides var. *robbiae*, see p.34
Geranium macrorrhizum, see p.83
Iris foetidissima var. *citrina*, see p.35
Lamium galeobdolon 'Florentinum', see p.47
Narcissus spp. and cvs.
Oenothera speciosa 'Rosea', see p.21

Lysimachia punctata
LOOSESTRIFE
☼ ◑ 4-8 ↕3ft (1m) ↔24in (60cm)

A reliable, robust perennial with clumps of leafy, erect stems. In summer, the leaf axils are crowded with cup-shaped yellow flowers. Too invasive for beds or borders.

OTHER MEDIUM TO TALL PERENNIALS FOR WILD AREAS

Aster novae-angliae
Baptisia spp. and cvs.
Campanula rapunculoides
Campanula trachelium
Coreopsis tripteris
Dryopteris filix-mas
Echinacea purpurea
Hemerocallis spp. and cvs.
Leucanthemum x *superbum*
Myrrhis odorata, see p.49

Saponaria officinalis 'Rubra Plena'
SOAPWORT
☼ 2-8 ↕↔36in (90cm)

The creeping rootstock of this reliable and easily grown plant forms patches of leafy stems, crowned in summer with fragrant, double, rose-pink flower clusters.

Rumex sanguineus
BLOODY DOCK
☼ 6-8 ↕36in (90cm) ↔12in (30cm)

This tap-rooted dock is valued mainly for its rosetted, red- or purple-veined leaves. In autumn, erect stems first bear clusters of tiny green flowers, then brown fruits.

Symphytum orientale
WHITE COMFREY
☼ ◑ ● 4-7 ↕28in (70cm) ↔18in (45cm)

Nodding clusters of funnel-shaped white flowers open on the erect, little-branched stems of this hairy plant in late spring and early summer. It tolerates dry shade.

Vinca major subsp. *hirsuta*
GREATER PERIWINKLE
☼ ◑ 7-9 ↕18in (45cm) ↔indefinite

This vigorous, scrambling or creeping, evergreen perennial or subshrub produces narrow-lobed violet flowers as new shoots emerge in spring, and into summer.

Bulbs for Naturalizing

THERE ARE FEW SIGHTS more inspiring than a meadow or woodland floor studded with wildflowers, creating a carpet of color as far as the eye can see. In the garden, bulbs especially lend themselves to such displays, and there is a multitude of species and cultivars available for this purpose. For a natural effect, plant bulbs in scattered groups, arranged in a free-form pattern. When planting, allow enough space between the bulbs for spreading clumps or self-seeding.

Anemone pavonina
ANEMONE
☼ 8-10 ↕10in (25cm) ↔6in (15cm)

This feathery-leaved anemone produces glowing red flowers with a white ring and dark eye in spring. Plant in sunny, well-drained sites in short grass or in a border.

Camassia leichtlinii
CAMASSIA
☼ ◑ 3-8 ↕4½ft (1.3m) ↔4in (10cm)

Long spires of star-shaped, blue or white flowers rise in summer above the slender leaves. This is an easily grown bulb ideal for moist meadows or grassy sites.

Crocus vernus 'Jeanne d'Arc'
DUTCH CROCUS
☼ 3-9 ↕5in (12cm) ↔2in (5cm)

Attractive and reliable, this large-flowered crocus forms clumps of grassy leaves in borders or short grass. White flowers with orange stigmas are produced in spring.

OTHER BULBS FOR NATURALIZING IN SHADE

Anemone blanda
Arisarum proboscideum
Arum italicum 'Marmoratum', see p.135
Colchicum speciosum
Crocus kotschyanus
Crocus tommasinianus, see p.98
Cyclamen coum
Cyclamen hederifolium, see p.96
Eranthis hyemalis, see p.98
Erythronium oregonum
Galanthus elwesii, see p.39
Hyacinthoides non-scripta
Leucojum aestivum
Lilium pyrenaicum
Narcissus spp. and cvs.
Ornithogalum nutans
Puschkinia scilloides, see p.57
Scilla spp. and cvs.

Erythronium dens-canis
DOGTOOTH VIOLET
☼ ◑ 2-7 ↕6in (15cm) ↔4in (10cm)

The exquisite, pinkish purple flowers are poised above rosettes of fleshy, beautifully mottled leaves in spring. Excellent for use in short grass and in woodlands.

Fritillaria meleagris
CHECKERED LILY
☼ ◑ 4-8 ↕12in (30cm) ↔3in (8cm)

A charming bulb with narrow leaves and nodding, bell-shaped, checked flowers on slender stems in spring. It thrives in moist grass or planted beneath shrubs.

Galanthus nivalis
COMMON SNOWDROP
◑ 3-9 ↕↔4in (10cm)

Drifts of this familiar woodland snowdrop are a spectacular sight during early spring. It naturalizes readily by seed and division, and will tolerate sun if the soil is moist.

Hyacinthoides hispanica
SPANISH BLUEBELL
☼ ◐ 4-9 ↕16in (40cm) ↔4in (10cm)

This robust bulb forms large patches of shiny leaves with nodding blue, white, or pink flowers on strong stems in spring. It may be too vigorous for a small garden.

Lilium martagon
MARTAGON LILY
☼ ◐ 3-8 ↕6ft (2m) ↔10in (25cm)

An old and reliable lily for naturalizing in grass or in a border. The tall stems bear whorled leaves and panicles of nodding flowers in a variety of colors in summer.

Narcissus bulbocodium
HOOP-PETTICOAT DAFFODIL
☼ 6-9 ↕6in (15cm) ↔3in (8cm)

A real charmer with narrow, threadlike leaves and striking, funnel-shaped, pale yellow flowers in spring. It will thrive and seed itself on a moist, grassy, sloping site.

Nectaroscordum siculum
NECTAROSCORDUM
☼ ◐ 6-10 ↕4ft (1.2m) ↔4in (10cm)

In summer, tall, strong stems carry loose umbels of drooping, bell-shaped green flowers flushed with purple. The straw-colored seed capsules are also ornamental.

Tulipa sylvestris
TULIP
◐ 4-10 ↕18in (45cm) ↔4in (10cm)

This tulip is easily established in grassland or in open woodland, where it forms patches. Star-shaped yellow flowers open in spring, but are not always freely borne.

OTHER BULBS FOR NATURALIZING IN SUN

Allium flavum
Allium unifolium
Anemone canadensis
Camassia quamash
Chionodoxa gigantea
Chionodoxa luciliae, see p.90
Colchicum autumnale
Crocus spp. and cvs.
Gladiolus communis subsp. *byzantinus*, see p.33
Lilium canadense
Lilium lancifolium
Lilium superbum
Muscari spp. and cvs.
Narcissus spp. and cvs.
Sternbergia lutea
Tulipa fosteriana
Tulipa kaufmanniana

Perennials for Rock Gardens

SOME OF THE LOVELIEST and most satisfying flowering perennials are those suited to the well-drained conditions of a rock garden. Many of these plants have a carpeting habit and are excellent groundcovers. Others form small clumps or mounds and associate well with miniature bulbs, such as crocuses, scillas, and glory-of-the-snow (*Chionodoxa*).

Aethionema 'Warley Rose'
PERSIAN STONECRESS
☼ 4-9 ↕↔ 8in (20cm)

A handsome, shrubby perennial forming an evergreen mound of slender stems with narrow, blue-gray leaves. Its pink flowers are borne in late spring and early summer.

Anthyllis montana
ALPS ANTHYLLIS
☼ 6-9 ↕ 12in (30cm) ↔ 24in (60cm)

Small, rounded, cloverlike heads of pink to purple, white-tipped flowers cover the dense carpet of deeply divided, silky, gray-green leaves from spring to summer.

Dianthus 'Pike's Pink'
ALPINE PINK
☼ 5-8 ↕ 6in (15cm) ↔ 8in (20cm)

The low, evergreen cushion of narrow, blue-gray leaves is topped in summer by double pale pink flowers with darker pink centers. Flowers have a lovely clove scent.

OTHER PERENNIALS FOR ROCK GARDENS

Anthemis biebersteiniana
Armeria cespitosa
Armeria maritima
Eriogonum umbellatum
Euphorbia myrsinites
Hypericum kamtschaticum
Iris pumila
Linaria alpina
Phlox subulata and cvs.
Potentilla nitida

Anemone sylvestris
SNOWDROP ANEMONE
☼ ☀ 3-8 ↕↔ 12in (30cm)

This low-grower forms patches of deeply cut, ferny leaves. Pure white flowers with gold stamens are borne in spring and early summer followed by silky seedheads.

Campanula carpatica 'Chewton Joy'
CARPATHIAN BELLFLOWER
☼ ☀ 3-8 ↕ 12in (30cm) ↔ 20in (50cm)

Low, trailing stems clothed with toothed, heart-shaped leaves bear upturned, bell-shaped blue flowers with paler centers for several months during summer.

Diascia 'Blackthorn Apricot'
DIASCIA
☼ 8-10 ↕ 10in (25cm) ↔ 20in (50cm)

This is a handsome new diascia cultivar. In summer, it bears abundant slender racemes of attractive apricot flowers above the mat or carpet of trailing green stems.

OTHER PERENNIALS FOR ROCK GARDENS

Aubrieta deltoidea
Helianthemum nummularium and cvs.
Houstonia caerulea
Lewisia Cotyledon Hybrids, see p.59
Lewisia rediviva
Lithodora diffusa 'Heavenly Blue'
Oxalis enneaphylla
Potentilla aurea
Saxifraga spp. and cvs.
Tanakaea radicans

Gentiana sino-ornata
AUTUMN GENTIAN
☼ ☀ 5-7 PH ↕3in (7cm) ↔12in (30cm)

This is one of the most striking autumn-flowering gentians. It produces an overwintering mat of trailing, leafy stems and upturned, deep blue trumpet flowers.

Gypsophila repens 'Rosa Schönheit'
CREEPING BABY'S-BREATH
☼ 3-8 ↕8in (20cm) ↔20in (50cm)

The semievergreen mat of slender, bluish green stems and leaves is smothered for many weeks during summer by tiny pink flowers. Also known as 'Pink Beauty'.

Geranium cinereum 'Ballerina'
GRAYLEAF CRANESBILL
☼ ☀ 4-10 ↕6in (15cm) ↔12in (30cm)

A neat little perennial producing a loose mound of small, gray-green leaves. Pale purplish red flowers with dark veins and eyes appear over a long period in summer.

Oxalis adenophylla
ALPINE OXALIS
☼ 7-11 ↕4in (10cm) ↔6in (15cm)

The tuft of deeply divided, grayish green leaves is accompanied during spring by funnel-shaped, purplish pink flowers with pale centers and dark throats.

Roscoea cautleoides 'Kew Beauty'
ROSCOEA
☼ ☀ 7-9 ↕16in (40cm) ↔6in (15cm)

Appearing in late spring, this gorgeous perennial produces a small clump of erect, leafy stems that carry loose spikes of large, pale yellow, orchidlike flowers.

Bulbs for Rock Gardens

Rock gardens and raised beds are excellent sites for growing the many miniature bulbs available. They are also ideal for larger bulbous plants that like well-drained, gritty soil and full sun. Most of the following are hardy and should be planted in groups or drifts for best effect. All will also thrive in containers, or in a scree garden – a well-drained bed with soil heavily amended with grit or fine gravel and mulched with additional gravel.

Allium narcissiflorum
Ornamental Onion
☼ 4-9 ↕12in (30cm) ↔ 2in (5cm)

Clusters of nodding, bell-shaped, red-purple or pale pink flowers are borne on upright stems in summer. The grasslike, grayish green leaves form a small clump.

Colchicum kesselringii
Colchicum
☼ 5-9 ↕↔ 1¼in (3cm)

Ideal for a sheltered, well-drained pocket, this lovely bulb bears white flowers like a miniature crocus in late winter and spring. The petals have purple-striped backs.

Chionodoxa forbesii
Glory-of-the-Snow
☼ 3-9 ↕8in (20cm) ↔ 4in (10cm)

A free-flowering, reliable bulb forming small tufts of narrow green leaves. In early spring, it produces loose clusters of lovely star-shaped blue flowers with white eyes.

Crocus chrysanthus 'E.A. Bowles'
Crocus
☼ 3-8 ↕3in (7cm) ↔ 2in (5cm)

This popular, spring-flowering crocus produces slender green leaves and lemon-yellow flowers, each with a bronze-green base and purple feathering on the outside.

Eucomis autumnalis
Pineapple Lily
☼ 8-10 ↕12in (30cm) ↔ 8in (20cm)

Fleshy stems bear crowded, green-white flower spikes from late summer to autumn above bold clumps of broad, strap-shaped, wavy-edged leaves. Likes a sheltered site.

Fritillaria pallidiflora
Fritillaria
☼ 5-8 ↕16in (40cm) ↔ 3in (7.5cm)

During late spring and early summer, this handsome bulb bears nodding, creamy yellow bell-shaped flowers from the axils of long, narrow, bloomy, gray-green leaves.

Other Bulbs for Rock Gardens

Allium beesianum
Allium moly, see p.38
Colchicum autumnale
Fritillaria meleagris, see p.52
Iris bucharica
Iris magnifica
Ixiolirion tataricum
Narcissus biflorus
Tulipa kaufmanniana
Tulipa humilis 'Violacea'

Iris danfordiae
DANFORD IRIS
☼ 5-9 ↕ 4in (10cm) ↔ 2in (5cm)

One of the most beautiful early bulbs, this miniature iris produces slim, four-angled leaves and yellow flowers with greenish yellow markings in late winter and spring.

OTHER MINIATURE BULBS FOR ROCK GARDENS

Allium mairei
Allium oreophilum
Crocus biflorus
Crocus chrysanthus
Iris reticulata
Muscari comosum
Narcissus bulbocodium var. *conspicuus*
Narcissus triandrus
Ornithogalum collinum
Tulipa batalinii

Scilla bifolia
SCILLA
☼ 3-8 ↕ 6in (15cm) ↔ 2in (5cm)

An easily grown bulb that increases very rapidly. It bears two narrow green leaves and loose sprays of star-shaped, blue to purple-blue flowers during early spring.

Narcissus minor
MINIATURE DAFFODIL
☼ 5-9 ↕ 5in (12.5cm) ↔ 3in (7.5cm)

This little daffodil forms tufts or patches of narrow, gray-green leaves. The inclined, small, trumpet-shaped yellow flowers are carried above the foliage in early spring.

Puschkinia scilloides
PUSCHKINIA
☼ 3-9 ↕ 6in (15cm) ↔ 3in (7.5cm)

Cheerful and reliable, this perennial soon forms a small clump of slender leaves accompanied in spring by clusters of very pale blue flowers with darker blue stripes.

Tulipa aucheriana
TULIP
☼ 4-7 ↕ 10in (25cm) ↔ 6in (15cm)

Starry pink flowers with yellow centers and stamens are borne singly or in twos or threes during spring. The narrow, bloomy green leaves are also attractive.

Perennials for Wall or Rock Crevices and Paving

ROCK CREVICES ARE the favored habitat of a wide range of attractive perennials, many of which have carpeting or trailing stems or form small rosettes or mounds. In the garden, these plants, which require well-drained soil, can be grown in the cracks of a dry stone wall or between paving slabs, where they will get the good drainage they need.

Asarina procumbens
ASARINA
☼ ◑ 6-8 ↕ 2in (5cm) ↔ 24in (60cm)

This semievergreen trailer has hairy stems and produces pale yellow, snapdragon-like flowers from the axils of its grayish green, kidney-shaped leaves during summer.

Aubrieta 'J.S. Baker'
AUBRETIA
☼ 4-8 ↕ 2in (5cm) ↔ 24in (60cm)

Aubretias are among the most colorful and reliable evergreen perennials for walls or rock-work. This one is smothered with purple, white-eyed flowers during spring.

Aurinia saxatilis 'Dudley Nevill'
BASKET-OF-GOLD
☼ 3-7 ↕ 8in (20cm) ↔ 12in (30cm)

A popular, clump-forming, woody-based plant with evergreen, gray-green leaves and clusters of tiny, soft yellow-buff flowers from late spring to early summer.

Campanula carpatica 'Jewel'
CARPATHIAN BELLFLOWER
☼ ◑ 3-8 ↕ 4in (10cm) ↔ 18in (45cm)

The small, dense, heart-shaped leaves of this popular and attractive compact bell-flower are almost hidden by its upturned, bright purple-blue blooms in summer.

Convolvulus sabatius
CONVOLVULUS
☼ 7-9 ↕ 6in (15cm) ↔ 24in (60cm)

The trailing, leafy stems of this carpeting, fast-growing perennial are studded with pale to deep lavender-blue flowers over many weeks during summer and autumn.

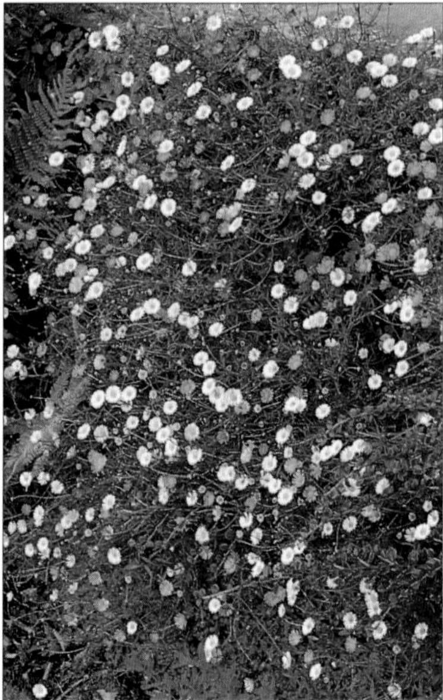

Erigeron karvinskianus
MEXICAN FLEABANE
☼ 5-7 ↕ 12in (30cm) ↔ 3ft (1m)

In summer, a succession of little white daisies, which fade to pink then to purple, smother this charming perennial's loose clump of slender, branching, leafy stems.

HERBACEOUS PERENNIALS FOR WALLS OR PAVING

Aethionema iberideum
Anthemis biebersteiniana
Campanula 'Birch Hybrid'
Erinus alpinus
Eriogonum umbellatum
Erodium chrysanthum
Hypericum kamtschaticum
Mazus reptans
Saponaria ocymoides 'Rubra Compacta'
Viola tricolor

Gypsophila repens 'Dorothy Teacher'
CREEPING BABY'S-BREATH
☼ 3-8 ↕2in (5cm) ↔16in (40cm)

Slender, crowded stems carpet the ground with small, narrow, blue-green leaves. The mass of beautiful, tiny, pale pink flowers borne in summer darkens with age.

EVERGREEN AND SEMIEVERGREEN PERENNIALS FOR WALLS OR PAVING

Antennaria dioica
Armeria maritima
Corydalis lutea, see p.82
Dianthus gratianopolitanus
Erigeron glaucus
Euphorbia myrsinites
Lithodora diffusa 'Heavenly Blue'
Phlox subulata
Sempervivum spp. and cvs.
Thymus pseudolanuginosus

Helianthemum 'Wisley White'
ROCKROSE, SUNROSE
☼ 5-10 ↕10in (25cm) ↔18in (45cm)

This woody-based evergreen perennial bears gray-green leaves and creamy white, yellow-centered flowers over a long period from late spring into midsummer.

Saxifraga 'Southside Seedling'
SAXIFRAGE
☼ ☀ 4-6 ↕12in (30cm) ↔8in (20cm)

The bold, arching sprays of red-spotted white flowers appear during late spring and early summer above the basal rosette of evergreen leaves. Also good in a trough.

Haberlea rhodopensis 'Virginalis'
HABERLEA
☼ ☀ 5-7 PH ↕6in (15cm) ↔10in (25cm)

Loose umbels of funnel-shaped white flowers top the dense, evergreen clump of hairy, coarse-toothed leaves in late spring and summer. Charming for a shady wall.

Lewisia Cotyledon Hybrids
LEWISIA
☼ ☀ 5-9 PH ↕10in (25cm) ↔12in (30cm)

From late spring to early summer, loose heads of attractive, magenta-pink, yellow, or orange flowers rise above the rosette of thick, wavy-margined, evergreen leaves.

Verbascum dumulosum
MULLEIN
☼ 6-10 ↕10in (25cm) ↔16in (40cm)

An evergreen, woody-based perennial that produces downy, gray-green stems and leaves. A succession of rich yellow flowers is borne during late spring and summer.

Perennials for Bog Gardens and Waterside Areas

A wealth of ornamental perennials are available for those fortunate enough to have water in their garden, even if it is only a wet, muddy depression. These plants rely on a constant supply of moisture for top performance. They include perennials that bear large or colorful flowers as well as those with bold or even variegated foliage.

Iris laevigata
Rabbit-ear Iris
5-9 ↕32in (80cm) ↔8in (20cm)

A handsome iris from Japan with erect, gray-green leaves and single lavender-blue, purple, or white flowers produced in summer. It will grow in shallow water.

Other Foliage Perennials for Bog & Waterside Gardens

Acorus calamus 'Variegatus'
Ajuga reptans 'Multicolor, see p.16
Carex elata 'Aurea', see p.128
Gunnera manicata
Hosta spp. and cvs.
Iris pseudacorus 'Variegata', see p.116
Lysimachia numularia 'Aurea', see p.128
Matteuccia struthiopteris, see p.65
Petasites japonicus var. *giganteus*

Astilbe 'Purpurlanze'
Astilbe
3-8 ↕4ft (1.2m) ↔36in (90cm)

The English name 'Purple Lance' aptly describes the stiff, purple-pink flower panicles of this late-flowering astilbe. Its deeply divided leaves form bold clumps.

Filipendula palmata 'Rubra'
Siberian Meadowsweet
3-8 ↕4ft (1.2m) ↔24in (60cm)

Sometimes confused with *F. rubra*, this stately, clump-forming perennial produces boldly lobed or divided leaves and dense plumes of tiny, rose-red summer flowers.

Darmera peltata
Umbrella Plant
5-7 ↕3½ft (1.1m) ↔30in (75cm)

This handsome perennial has creeping rhizomes that form a large patch of long-stalked leaves, coloring richly in autumn. Pink flowerheads are produced in spring.

Hosta 'Zounds'
Hosta
3-9 ↕22in (55cm) ↔3ft (1m)

Striking and also relatively slug-proof, this hosta develops a bold clump of corrugated leaves. White flowers appear in summer and the yellow-green foliage ages to gold.

Lysichiton americanus
Yellow Skunk Cabbage
4-8 ↕3ft (1m) ↔4ft (1.2m)

A spectacular, easily recognized perennial that bears large yellow flowers in spring followed by huge paddle-shaped leaves. It will grow in moist soil or standing water.

Oenanthe javanica 'Flamingo'
WATER DROPWORT
☼ ☀ 9-11 ↕16in (40cm) ↔36in (90cm)

The deeply cut, green-and-white leaves of this creeping, fleshy-stemmed plant are flushed with pink in autumn. Small white flowerheads emerge in late summer.

Osmunda regalis
ROYAL FERN
☼ ☀ 3-9 ↕5ft (1.5m) ↔4ft (1.2m)

An impressive fern forming a bold clump of deeply divided fronds that often color richly in autumn before dying. It produces spikes of red-brown spores in summer.

Primula prolifera
CANDELABRA PRIMROSE
☼ ☀ 6-8 ↕24in (60cm) ↔6in (15cm)

In early summer, slender, erect stems with many whorls of yellow flowers rise above the basal rosettes of deep green leaves. It is excellent for planting in large drifts.

Rheum palmatum 'Bowles Crimson'
ORNAMENTAL RHUBARB
☼ ☀ 5-9 ↕8ft (2.5m) ↔6ft (1.8m)

The big, jaggedly lobed leaves of this spectacular perennial emerge crimson and form a giant clump. Statuesque panicles of red flowers are produced in early summer.

Rodgersia pinnata
RODGERSIA
☼ ☀ 5-8 ↕4ft (1.2m) ↔30in (75cm)

Superb for both foliage and flowers, with deeply divided, veined leaves, tinted red in autumn and spring. The frothy white flower plumes appear during summer.

SPECIFIC USES

OTHER FLOWERING PERENNIALS FOR BOG & WATERSIDE GARDENS

Euphorbia palustris
Eupatorium purpureum 'Atropurpureum', see p.18
Filipendula purpurea, see p.122
Iris ensata and cvs.
Kirengeshoma palmata, see p.109
Ligularia spp. and cvs.
Lobelia cardinalis and cvs.
Lysichiton camtschatcensis
Primula japonica

Zantedeschia aethiopica 'Crowborough'
CALLA LILY
☼ ☀ 7-11 ↕36in (90cm) ↔24in (60cm)

This handsome perennial has large, arrow-shaped leaves and beautiful, long-stalked white flowers in summer. It will grow in either moist soil or shallow water.

Aquatic Perennials

THERE ARE VERY FEW RICHER, or more ornamental, wildlife habitats in the garden than in and around a well-planted pond. Marginal perennials, as well as those that prefer deeper water, will attract a range of birds, insects, and other wildlife. Large ponds offer the most scope for planting, but water can be introduced into even a small backyard. Planting advice below gives optimum water depth; plant heights are from water level.

Aponogeton distachyos
WATER HAWTHORN
☼ ☀ 9-10 ↕3in (7.5cm) ↔4ft (1.2m)

In spring and autumn, curious spikes of vanilla-scented white flowers rise above the floating, semievergreen, oblong leaves. Plant in water 12–24in (30–60cm) deep.

Houttuynia cordata 'Chameleon'
HOUTTUYNIA
☼ ☀ 5-8 ↕12in (30cm) ↔indefinite

Handsome leaves are variegated with pale yellow, green, and red. A fast-spreading marginal aquatic, ideal for water to 4in (10cm) deep. Quite invasive in moist soil.

Nymphaea 'Firecrest'
WATER LILY
☼ 3-11 ↕3in (7.5cm) ↔4ft (1.2m)

This water lily's rounded, floating leaves are purple when young. Its fragrant pink flowers open in summer. Ideal for a small pond. Plant 6–18in (15–45cm) deep.

Nymphaea 'Gladstoniana'
WATER LILY
☼ 3-11 ↕3in (7.5cm) ↔8ft (2.4m)

This popular, vigorous water lily has starry white summer flowers. The wavy-edged, rounded, floating leaves are bronze when young. Plant 45–90cm (18–36in) deep.

Butomus umbellatus
FLOWERING RUSH
☼ 5-7 ↕4ft (1.2m) ↔18in (45cm)

A robust plant for pond margins forming a patch of grassy, three-cornered leaves. Tall stems bear umbels of rose-pink flowers in summer. Plant 3–5in (7–13cm) deep.

Nymphaea 'Chromatella'
WATER LILY
☼ 3-11 ↕3in (7.5cm) ↔5ft (1.5m)

Free-flowering and vigorous, this reliable plant has beautiful, canary yellow flowers in summer and bronze-splashed floating leaves. Plant 18–36in (45–90cm) deep.

Nymphoides peltata
FLOATING HEART
☼ 6-10 ↕3in (7.5cm) ↔indefinite

Ideal for a large pond, this fast-spreader has rounded, floating leaves and golden, funnel-shaped, fringe-petaled flowers in summer. Plant 12–24in (30–60cm) deep.

Orontium aquaticum
GOLDEN CLUB
☼ 6-11 ↕12in (30cm) ↔24in (60cm)

A vigorous, native marginal aquatic with oblong, blue-green leaves. Curved white stalks bear yellow flower spikes in spring. Plant 12–16in (30–40cm) deep.

Pontederia cordata
PICKEREL WEED
☼ 3-11 ↕30in (75cm) ↔24in (60cm)

From summer to early fall, spikes of blue flowers poke through the clumps of erect, glossy leaves. Plant this vigorous marginal 3–5in (7–13cm) deep, or in very moist soil.

Stratiotes aloides
WATER SOLDIER
☼ 6-9 ↕6in (15cm) ↔8in (20cm)

Pineapple-like rosettes of saw-toothed leaves rise to the water surface in summer as the erect, three-petaled white flowers are borne. Plant 12–36in (30–90cm) deep.

Sagittaria latifolia
ARROWHEAD, DUCK POTATO
☼ 4-11 ↕↔36in (90cm)

A tuberous marginal aquatic with slender, triangular stems and arrow-shaped, long-stalked leaves. In summer, whorls of white flowers open. Plant 3–5in (7–13cm) deep.

OTHER AQUATIC PERENNIALS

Acorus calamus
Acorus gramineus
Alisma plantago-aquatica
Calla palustris
Hydrocotyle verticillata
Iris laevigata, see p.60
Iris pseudacorus
Iris versicolor
Lysichiton spp.
Marsilea mutica
Menyanthes trifoliata
Myriophyllum verticillatum
Nelumbo nucifera
Nymphaea spp. and cvs.
Peltandra virginica
Sagittaria sagittifolia
Saururus cernuus
Thalia dealbata
Typha laxmannii

Typha minima
MINIATURE CATTAIL
☼ 3-11 ↕30in (75cm) ↔18in (45cm)

A rushlike marginal aquatic with slender leaves. The stems of brown flowerheads in summer turn into fluffy seedheads in winter. Plant 2–4in (5–10cm) deep.

Perennials for Containers in Sun

ONE OF THE MAIN ADVANTAGES of growing perennials in containers is that they can easily be moved around the garden or patio, just like furniture inside the house. Containers also allow less hardy plants, like some of the sun-lovers below, to be grown outdoors for summer effect, then moved under cover for protection in winter.

Agapanthus 'Loch Hope'
AFRICAN LILY
☼ 7-10 ↕ 4ft (1.2m) ↔ 24in (60cm)

This bold, clump-forming perennial has slender, grayish green leaves. Deep blue trumpet-shaped flowers are borne in loose heads from late summer into autumn.

Argyranthemum 'Jamaica Primrose'
MARGUERITE
☼ 9-11 ↕↔ 3ft (1m)

A bushy evergreen, grown as an annual, with fernlike, gray-green leaves. Its long-stalked, primrose yellow daisies are borne over a long period from spring to autumn.

Canna 'Assaut'
INDIAN SHOT
☼ 7-11 ↕ 5ft (1.5m) ↔ 20in (50cm)

A striking tender perennial with purple-brown leaves and erect, leafy stems that bear heads of gladiolus-like, orange-scarlet flowers in summer and autumn.

Eucomis bicolor
PINEAPPLE FLOWER
☼ 8-11 ↕ 18in (45cm) ↔ 12in (30cm)

Dense, erect spikes of pale green, purple-edged flowers with pineapple-like crowns rise above the broad, strap-shaped, fleshy leaves during late summer.

Osteospermum 'Silver Sparkler'
OSTEOSPERMUM
☼ 9-11 ↕ 24in (60cm) ↔ 18in (45cm)

This vigorous, bushy plant has creamy white-margined leaves. Dark shoots bear long-stalked white daisy flowers, darker on the reverse, from summer into autumn.

TENDER PERENNIALS FOR CONTAINERS IN SUN

Agapanthus spp. and cvs.
Anisodontea x *hypomadarum*
Brugmansia x *candida*
Cortaderia selloana 'Pumila', see p.28
Cosmos atrosanguineus
Helichrysum petiolare
Heliotropium arborescens
Lavandula stoechas, see p.73
Lotus berthelotii
Pelargonium spp. and cvs.

Verbena x *hybrida* 'Peaches and Cream'
VERBENA
☼ 8-10 ↕ 18in (45cm) ↔ 20in (50cm)

Domed heads of pale orange-pink flowers, which age to apricot then creamy yellow, cover the mound of toothed, dark green, roughly-hairy leaves from summer to fall.

Perennials for Containers in Shade

SHADY PATIOS, BACKYARDS, and similar sunless situations, particularly when paved or close to the house, are not always the easiest places to accommodate plants unless they are grown in containers. Foliage perennials are especially useful in shade and are striking in containers either used as specimens or arranged in groups.

OTHER PERENNIALS FOR CONTAINERS IN SHADE

Bergenia cordifolia 'Purpurea', see p.114
Dryopteris erythrosora, see p.140
Hakonechloa macra 'Aureola', see p.124
Helleborus argutifolius, see p.114
Heuchera spp. and cvs.
Hosta spp. and cvs.
Lilium longiflorum
Saxifraga stolonifera, see p.35
Tolmiea menziesii 'Taff's Gold', see p.125

Aspidistra elatior
ASPIDISTRA, CAST-IRON PLANT
☀☀ 7-11 ↕↔ 24in (60cm)

A houseplant in northern zones, this easy-to-grow plant forms handsome, evergreen clumps of broad, strap-shaped, beautifully veined and glossy foliage.

Hosta 'Sum and Substance'
HOSTA
☀☀ 3-9 ↕ 30in (75cm) ↔ 36in (90cm)

One of the best hostas for brightening a shady corner with bold clumps of heart-shaped, yellow-green to yellow leaves. It bears pale lilac flowers in summer.

Matteucia struthiopteris
OSTRICH FERN
☀ 2-6 ↕ 4ft (1.2m) ↔ 20in (50cm)

The bold, elegant clumps of featherlike fronds surround a central cluster of dark brown, spore-bearing fronds from late summer onward. It needs moist, rich soil.

Corydalis flexuosa
'China Blue'
☀ 5-8 ↕ 10in (25cm) ↔ 8in (20cm)

Worth growing just for its attractive, ferny, mounds of bright green foliage, which die down in early summer as the racemes of tubular, striking blue flowers fade.

Liriope muscari
LILYTURF
☀☀ 6-8 ↕ 12in (30cm) ↔ 18in (45cm)

Dense tufts of evergreen, strap-shaped, dark green leaves are joined in autumn by stiff, crowded spikes of small violet-mauve flowers. An excellent groundcover too.

Rodgersia pinnata 'Superba'
RODGERSIA
☼☀☀ 5-8 ↕ 4ft (1.2m) ↔ 30in (75cm)

This vigorous clump-former has the dual attractions of bold, fingered, veiny leaves, bronze-purple when young, and conical, rich pink flower plumes in summer.

Climbing Perennials

Most climbing perennials cultivated in the garden are woody-stemmed and have a permanent presence above ground. However, there are also herbaceous perennials that have twining or scrambling stems suitable for clothing walls, fences, and trellises, or for training over shrubs or similar supports. Some of these climbers also offer decorative fruits and seedheads, or leaves that are attractively and richly tinted during autumn.

Other Climbing Perennials

- *Aconitum hemsleyanum*
- *Aconitum volubile*
- *Apios americana*
- *Aster carolinianus*
- *Calystegia hederacea* 'Flore Pleno'
- *Clematis* x *eriostemon*
- *Dioscorea batatus*
- *Lathyrus latifolius*, see p.50
- *Lathyrus rotundifolius*
- *Passiflora caerulea*
- *Tropaeolum tuberosum*

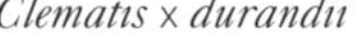

Clematis x *durandii*
Clematis
☼ 6-9 ↕ 6ft (2m) ↔ 3ft (1m)

Excellent as a groundcover or for training over a small bush, the slender stems bear summer flowers with creamy stamens and wide-spaced, indigo blue tepals.

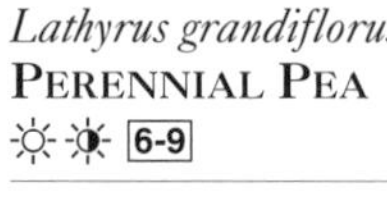

Lathyrus grandiflorus
Perennial Pea
☼ ☀ 6-9 ↕↔ 5ft (1.5m)

An old cottage-garden favorite providing dense cover with its rampant, slender stems. Long-stalked clusters of pink, red, and purple flowers are borne in summer.

Humulus lupulus 'Aureus'
Golden Hop
☼ ☀ 6-9 ↕↔ 20ft (6m)

The twining stems of this fast-growing, vigorous climber blanket its support with golden yellow leaves. Bunches of greenish yellow seedheads are produced in autumn.

Lathyrus latifolius 'Albus'
Perennial Pea
☼ ☀ 6-9 ↕↔ 6ft (2m)

Easy and reliable, this scrambler is ideal for a wall or hedge, or for covering a steep bank. In summer and autumn, it produces pea-shaped, pure white flowers.

Tropaeolum speciosum
Vermilion Nasturtium
☼ ☀ 7-9 PH ↕↔ 10ft (3m)

Spectacular when in flower in summer and autumn, the long-spurred, flame red blooms are followed by small blue fruits with red collars. It needs cool, moist soil.

Perennials with Leaves for Cutting

IN THE HOME, AS IN THE GARDEN, foliage is as important and decorative as flowers. Many perennials can provide a regular and reliable supply of attractive leaves for cutting whenever required. Useful for adding a green, gray, or golden foil to flower arrangements, cut leaves will also make an effective display by themselves.

Paeonia 'Edulis Superba'
PEONY
☼ ☀ 2-8 ↕↔ 36in (90cm)

Most herbaceous peonies have attractive, dark green foliage with contrasting red or purplish stalks. This one also has double pink flowers that are excellent for cutting.

Hosta 'Hadspen Blue'
HOSTA
☀ ● 3-9 ↕ 10in (25cm) ↔ 24in (60cm)

Hostas are invaluable for cut foliage and those with blue-gray leaves are especially useful. This exceptional example provides handsome, bold, heart-shaped leaves.

OTHER PERENNIALS WITH LEAVES FOR CUTTING

Artemisia ludoviciana
Arum italicum 'Marmoratum', see p.135
Astilbe spp. and cvs.
Bergenia cordifolia 'Purpurea', see p.114
Hakonechloa macra 'Aureola', see p.124
Heuchera americana and cvs.
Lavandula angustifolia
Polystichum spp. and cvs.
Rodgersia pinnata, see p.61
Vinca minor 'Gertrude Jekyll', see p.47

Hosta 'Green Fountain'
HOSTA
☀ ● 3-9 ↕ 18in (45cm) ↔ 3ft (1m)

This hosta's arching, lance-shaped leaves are glossy and wavy-margined. Ideal for picking, they form a bold clump. Arching stems bear pale mauve flowers in summer.

Iris pallida 'Argentea Variegata'
VARIEGATED SWEET IRIS
☼ ☀ 4-8 ↕ 32in (80cm) ↔ 24in (60cm)

One of the most spectacular variegated perennials with sword-shaped, boldly margined leaves lasting long into autumn. Fragrant flowers appear in early summer.

Polygonatum falcatum 'Variegatum'
SOLOMON'S SEAL
☼ ☀ 5-8 ↕ 24in (60cm) ↔ 12in (30cm)

This charming perennial forms a clump of arching reddish shoots with rich green, cream-margined leaves. In spring, it bears clusters of pendent, bell-shaped flowers.

Perennials for Cut Flowers

HAVING FLOWERS AVAILABLE for cutting is one of the most enjoyable bonuses of growing perennials in the garden. Cut selectively, preferably from well-established perennials, to ensure that the plants remain well-shaped, attractive, and vigorous. Although some perennials, like chrysanthemums, have long been popular among florists, many more produce flowers suitable for cutting. Once cut, stand the flowers in a deep container filled with luke warm water overnight before use.

Aquilegia McKana Hybrids
COLUMBINE
☼ ☀ 3-9 ↕30in (75cm) ↔24in (60cm)

This striking but short-lived perennial produces its attractive, large, long-spurred flowers in shades of blue, yellow, and red from late spring through to midsummer.

OTHER SPRING AND EARLY SUMMER FLOWERS FOR CUTTING

Baptisia australis, see p.92
Convallaria majalis
Hyacinthoides hispanica, see p.53
Iris sibirica and cvs.
Leucojum aestivum 'Gravetye Giant', see p.39
Narcissus spp. and cvs.
Thermopsis caroliniana
Tulipa spp. and cvs.
Viola odorata and cvs.

Aster x *frikartii* 'Wunder von Stäfa'
FRIKART'S ASTER
☼ 5-8 ↕28in (70cm) ↔16in (40cm)

A reliable perennial for a late summer or early autumn border with a multitude of long-lasting blue, orange-centered daisies. Its stems may flop if not given support.

Astilbe 'Professor van der Wielen'
ASTILBE
☼ ☀ 3-9 ↕4ft (1.2m) ↔3ft (1m)

In summer, tall, arching plumes of tiny white flowers rise over mounds of much-divided leaves. One of the boldest and most satisfying astilbes for cool, moist soil.

Catananche caerulea
CUPID'S DART
☼ 4-9 ↕32in (80cm) ↔12in (30cm)

The slender clusters of erect, wiry stems are tipped in summer with papery, pearly white buds, opening to blue flowers. The flowers are also attractive when dried.

Gaillardia x *grandiflora* 'Kobold'
BLANKET FLOWER
☼ 4-9 ↕12in (30cm) ↔18in (45cm)

This showy but short-lived, bushy plant bears an abundance of large, brilliant red, yellow-tipped daisy flowers on leafy stems during summer and early autumn.

Iris unguicularis 'Mary Barnard'
WINTER IRIS
☼ 7-9 ↕12in (30cm) ↔24in (60cm)

The fragrant, solitary flowers of this sun-loving iris appear from late winter to early spring and are best picked when in bud. Its evergreen leaves form a grassy clump.

Leucanthemum × *superbum* 'Cobham Gold'
☼ ◐ 4-8 ↕24in (60cm) ↔8in (20cm)

This lovely selection is one of the Shasta daisies, which are all excellent for cutting. It forms robust clumps with double white flowers during summer and early autumn.

Liatris spicata 'Kobold'
SPIKE GAYFEATHER
☼ 3-9 ↕20in (50cm) ↔18in (45cm)

Erect, dense spikes of purple flowers open in late summer and autumn above clumps of slender leaves. A striking and reliable perennial for moist but well-drained soils.

Lilium 'African Queen'
TRUMPET LILY
☼ ◐ 4-8 ↕5ft (1.5m) ↔12in (30cm)

Most lilies are good for cutting, and this is no exception. Its tall stems bear narrow, crowded leaves and terminal umbels of fragrant, nodding flowers in summer.

OTHER SUMMER FLOWERS FOR CUTTING

Achillea spp. and cvs.
Campanula persicifolia and cvs.
Crocosmia masoniorum, see p.104
Delphinium spp. and cvs.
Dianthus 'Doris', see p.110
Echinacea purpurea and cvs.
Gypsophila paniculata 'Bristol Fairy', see p.93
Phlox paniculata and cvs.
Platycodon grandiflorus, see p.77

Paeonia officinalis 'Crimson Globe'
PEONY
☼ 3-8 ↕34in (85cm) ↔36in (90cm)

This bold, clump-forming peony produces handsome, divided, deep green foliage. It bears large, garnet red blooms with golden stamens in late spring or early summer.

Schizostylis coccinea 'Viscountess Byng'
KAFFIR LILY
☼ 7-9 ↕24in (60cm) ↔12in (30cm)

A very useful autumn-flowering perennial forming dense clumps of narrow, irislike leaves and bearing graceful, loose spikes of star-shaped, pale pink flowers.

Solidago 'Laurin'
GOLDENROD
☼ 4-9 ↕30in (75cm) ↔18in (45cm)

This compact version of an old-fashioned, cottage-garden stalwart carries branched, spreading heads of deep yellow flowers on clumps of leafy stems during late summer.

Perennials with Decorative Winter Seedheads

MOST GARDENERS NOW RECOGNIZE that taking too tidy an approach to the garden at the end of the growing season can rob them of some striking winter effects. Any perennial that ends the growing season with attractive seedheads can provide winter interest. Their architectural beauty will be further enhanced by a covering of snow or frost.

Achillea filipendulina
FERNLEAF YARROW
☼ 3-9 ↕ 4ft (1.2m) ↔ 18in (45cm)

The flattened seedheads of this clump-forming, stiff-stemmed perennial provide a ready platform for snow or frost. Its yellow flowers are produced in summer.

Echinops ritro
GLOBE THISTLE
☼ ◐ 3-8 ↕ 24in (60cm) ↔ 18in (45cm)

When covered in frost, the globular, spiky seedheads of this easy-to-grow perennial look like decorative baubles. The flowers emerge steely blue in early summer.

Miscanthus sinensis 'Kleine Fontäne'
MISCANTHUS
☼ 5-9 ↕ 5ft (1.5m) ↔ 4ft (1.2m)

In autumn, handsome clumps of tall, erect stems with narrow leaves bear fingerlike spikelets that turn fluffy and from buff to white in winter. Ideal for small gardens.

OTHER PERENNIALS WITH DECORATIVE WINTER SEEDHEADS

Astilbe spp. and cvs.
Baptisia australis, see p.92
Cimicifuga simplex
Echinacea purpurea
Eupatorium purpureum
Pennisetum alopecuroides
Rudbeckia spp. and cvs.
Sedum spectabile, see p.102
Thermopsis caroliniana

Chasmanthium latifolium
NORTHERN SEA OATS
☼ ◐ 5-9 ↕ 3ft (1m) ↔ 24in (60cm)

This gorgeous grass forms loose clumps of leafy stems. These bear drooping clusters of flattened, green or pink-tinted spikelets that turn pale brown during winter.

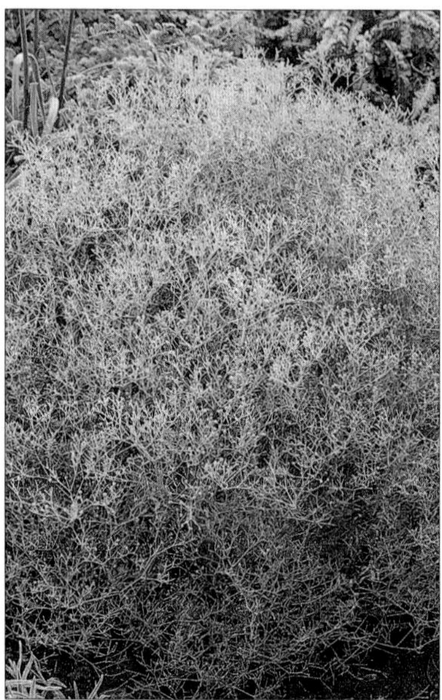

Gypsophila paniculata
'Compacta Plena'
☼ 3-9 ↕ 12in (30cm) ↔ 24in (60cm)

This dwarf, double-flowered baby's-breath produces small, soft pink to white flowers in summer. Its dried branches are attractive in winter when covered by frost.

Monarda 'Beauty of Cobham'
BEE BALM
☼ ◐ 3-9 ↕ 36in (90cm) ↔ 18in (45cm)

Flowering during late summer and early autumn, this lovely plant bears crowded heads of pink flowers, with purple bracts that turn a warm brown in winter.

Stipa tenuissima
Feather Grass
☼ 6-10 ↕↔ 24in (60cm)

A densely tufted grass with ever-moving, erect then arching stems. These bear long, feathery heads of green-white spikelets that turn a warm buff color during winter.

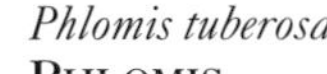

Phlomis tuberosa
Phlomis
☼ 5-8 ↕ 5ft (1.5m) ↔ 36in (90cm)

Two-lipped, rose-lilac flowers with reddish calyces are produced in summer. During winter, the striking clumps of tall, leafless stems carry dense brown seedheads.

Phlox 'Lichtspel'
Border Phlox
☼ 4-8 ↕ 4ft (1.2m) ↔ 24in (60cm)

During summer, the clumps of erect, leafy stems carry panicles of lilac-rose flowers. The stems and remaining flowerheads fade to a warm pale brown during winter.

Rhaponticum cynarioides
Rhaponticum
☼ 6-8 ↕ 30in (75cm) ↔ 12in (30cm)

Erect stems rise from a rosette of lobed leaves in summer to bear large cornflower-like heads of pink flowers that turn brown and persist throughout winter.

Veronicastrum virginicum
Culver's Root
☼ ◐ 3-9 ↕ 6ft (2m) ↔ 18in (45cm)

Tapered spikes of blue-purple flowers top dense clumps of erect stems with whorled leaves in summer and autumn. In winter, the spikes lengthen and turn brown.

Perennials Attractive to Bees, Butterflies, and Other Insects

BUTTERFLIES ARE ALWAYS WELCOME garden visitors, but many other less decorative insects have more important roles to play. These include bees, which are essential garden pollinators, and also hoverflies, whose larvae feed on aphids and other similar insects, acting as a natural method of pest control. They will all be attracted by the following perennials.

OTHER PERENNIALS ATTRACTIVE TO BEES AND BUTTERFLIES

Achillea spp. and cvs.
Asclepias tuberosa, see p.104
Aster novae-angliae and cvs.
Centranthus ruber, see p.86
Coreopsis lanceolata
Echinacea purpurea
Eupatorium purpureum
Mentha spp. and cvs.
Monarda didyma
Nepeta spp. and cvs.

Allium 'Purple Sensation'
ORNAMENTAL ONION
☼ 3-8 ↕36in (90cm) ↔4in (10cm)

All the alliums are attractive to insects, but this one is particularly impressive. The tall stems carry spangled globes of starry, deep violet flowers during summer.

Centaurea 'Pulchra Major'
CENTAUREA
☼ 3-8 ↕4ft (1.2m) ↔24in (60cm)

This bold clump-former has handsome, silver-gray foliage. During summer, erect, branching stems carry striking, rose-pink flowerheads with scaly, silvery bracts.

Calamintha nepeta 'White Cloud'
CALAMINT
☼ ☀ 5-9 ↕18in (45cm) ↔30in (75cm)

Bees especially love this small-flowered perennial. Throughout summer, the low mound of crowded, aromatic leaves is peppered with tiny, pure white blooms.

Cephalaria gigantea
GIANT SCABIOUS
☼ ☀ 3-8 ↕8ft (2.5m) ↔36in (90cm)

A special favorite with bees, this large perennial forms clumps of deeply lobed leaves and bears primrose yellow flowerheads on tall, branched stems in summer.

Doronicum pardalianches
LEOPARD'S BANE
☀ 4-8 ↕36in (90cm) ↔4ft (1.2m)

In time, this creeping perennial will form a substantial patch of heart-shaped, softly-hairy leaves. Yellow daisies are borne over a long period in spring and summer.

Echinops ritro 'Veitch's Blue'
Globe Thistle

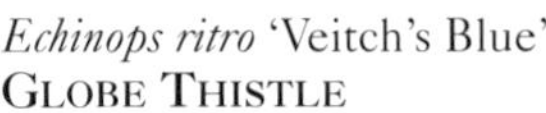

☼ ◐ 3-8 ↕4ft (1.2m) ↔30in (75cm)

During summer, the spherical, spiky blue flowerheads make this a favorite with both children and bees. Its spine-toothed, deep-cut leaves are white-downy beneath.

Inula hookeri
Inula

☼ 4-8 ↕↔36in (90cm)

In summer and autumn, the bold clumps of downy, leafy stems bear golden daisy flowers with threadlike petals from woolly buds. A striking plant, popular with bees.

Lavandula stoechas
French Lavender

☼ 7-9 ↕↔24in (60cm)

Bushy, with a dense, compact habit, this aromatic evergreen has narrow, gray-green leaves. Long-stalked spikes of purple flowers appear in late spring and summer.

Melittis melissophyllum
Bastard Balm

☼ ◐ 6-9 ↕↔12in (30cm)

This softly-downy plant has four-angled stems and honey-scented foliage. Loved by bees, the purple-lipped, white to pink flowers open in spring and early summer.

Salvia pratensis Haematodes Group
Meadow Sage

☼ ◐ 3-9 ↕36in (90cm) ↔12in (30cm)

Short-lived but free-seeding, this lovely sage produces large, branching heads of blue-violet flowers during summer above rosettes of large, aromatic green leaves.

Sedum 'Herbstfreude'
Showy Stonecrop

☼ 3-9 ↕↔24in (60cm)

Butterflies and bees cover the deep pink autumn flowers, which mature to copper-red. The fleshy leaves are grayish green. Commonly known as *S.* 'Autumn Joy'.

Solidago 'Goldenmosa'
Goldenrod

☼ 3-9 ↕3ft (1m) ↔24in (60cm)

A compact, bushy perennial with upright, leafy stems bearing conical heads of bright yellow flowers from late summer to fall. It is excellent for smaller gardens.

Perennials Tolerant of Air Pollution

CAR EXHAUST AND OTHER AIR POLLUTANTS can have a detrimental effect on all plants, and prolonged exposure may ultimately kill them. Fortunately, such cases are the exception rather than the rule. The following perennials can generally be relied upon to tolerate all but the most extreme conditions along roadsides, driveways, or industrial areas.

Leucanthemum x *superbum* 'Esther Read'

☼ 4-8 ↕↔ 24in (60cm)

The large, double, pure white flowerheads of this reliable, summer-blooming Shasta daisy are good for cutting. Its leafy stems form broad clumps.

Achillea ptarmica 'The Pearl'
SNEEZEWORT

☼ 2-9 ↕ 30in (75cm) ↔ 24in (60cm)

This tough favorite develops clumps of aromatic, narrow, toothy leaves. The dense heads of buttonlike white flowers are produced in summer. It reseeds freely.

Geranium pratense 'Plenum Caeruleum'

☼ ☀ 3-8 ↕ 36in (90cm) ↔ 24in (60cm)

All forms of this popular hardy geranium are reliable. This strong-growing selection produces attractive, small, loosely double, lavender-blue flowers during summer.

Lupinus 'My Castle'
LUPINE

☼ 3-6 ↕ 36in (90cm) ↔ 30in (75cm)

Spikes of pealike, rose-pink flowers top bold clumps of erect stems and finger-like leaves in summer. Lupines do not thrive in areas with hot, humid summers.

Aster novae-angliae 'Andenken an Alma Pötschke'

☼ ☀ 3-8 ↕ 4ft (1.2m) ↔ 24in (60cm)

Often known simply as 'Alma Pötschke', this clump-forming New England aster lights up the early autumn days with its brilliant salmon-pink daisy flowers.

Geum 'Lady Stratheden'
AVENS

☼ ☀ 4-7 ↕↔ 24in (60cm)

An old favorite and a contrast to scarlet *G.* 'Mrs. Bradshaw' bearing loose sprays of semidouble, rich yellow summer flowers and deeply divided, fresh green leaves.

OTHER FLOWERING PERENNIALS TOLERANT OF AIR POLLUTION

Anaphalis margaritacea, see p.78
Anemone x *hybrida*
Dicentra eximia and cvs.
Geranium x *magnificum*
Hemerocallis spp. and cvs.
Liatris spicata
Lychnis chalcedonica
Rudbeckia spp. and cvs.
Sidalcea candida
Solidago spp. and cvs.

Lupinus 'Noble Maiden'
LUPINE
☼ 3-6 ↕36in (90cm) ↔30in (75cm)

A lovely lupine with tapered racemes of creamy white, pealike flowers that rise in summer above clumps of divided foliage. Like most lupines, it is attractive to slugs.

Malva moschata
MUSK MALLOW
☼ 3-7 ↕36in (90cm) ↔24in (60cm)

Attractive and easily grown, this perennial forms clumps of finely divided, aromatic leaves. It bears racemes of pink hibiscus-like flowers from midsummer onward.

OTHER FOLIAGE PERENNIALS TOLERANT OF AIR POLLUTION

Artemisia ludoviciana 'Silver Queen', see p.86
Festuca glauca
Lamium galeobdolon
Miscanthus spp. and cvs.
Pennisetum alopecuroides
Sedum spp. and cvs.
Sempervivum spp. and cvs.
Stachys byzantina, see p.45
Yucca spp. and cvs.

Pentaglottis sempervirens
GREEN ALKANET
☀☀ 7-9 ↕36in (90cm) ↔24in (60cm)

The robust clump of overwintering, hairy leaves is topped in spring by erect, leafy stems bearing rich blue flowers. Excellent for planting along hedges or in woodlands.

Potentilla 'Gibson's Scarlet'
POTENTILLA
☼ 4-8 ↕18in (45cm) ↔24in (60cm)

This potentilla produces its bright scarlet blooms in summer above clumps of long-stalked, deeply divided leaves. Striking in flower and popular for use in borders.

Solidago 'Golden Wings'
GOLDENROD
☼ 3-9 ↕6ft (1.8m) ↔36in (90cm)

During late summer and autumn, the erect, leafy stems of this robust perennial are crowned with spreading, branched clusters of small, golden yellow flowers.

Veronica spicata 'Rotfuchs'
SPIKE SPEEDWELL
☼ 3-8 ↕↔12in (30cm)

During summer, erect, tapering spikes of eye-catching, deep pink flowers tower above the low clump of willowlike leaves. In English, its name means 'Red Fox'.

Perennials Tolerant of Coastal Exposure

EXPOSURE TO STRONG WINDS, SALT SPRAY, AND SUN are the three main features of life by the seaside. As the soil here is also often sandy and fast-draining, to survive plants must be robust and adaptable. A surprising number of perennials can cope successfully and even thrive in these conditions and are ideal for a coastal garden.

Allium giganteum
GIANT ONION
☼ 4-8 ↕5ft (1.5m) ↔6in (15cm)

Round heads of starry, lilac-pink flowers top the tall stems of this striking plant in summer. Its two strap-shaped, gray-green basal leaves wither before flowering.

Centaurea hypoleuca 'John Coutts'
KNAPWEED
☼ 3-7 ↕24in (60cm) ↔18in (45cm)

In summer, erect stems bear long-lasting, fragrant, deep rose-pink flowerheads above bold clumps of deeply lobed, wavy-edged leaves that are gray-white beneath.

Cichorium intybus 'Roseum'
CHICORY
☼ 3-10 ↕4ft (1.2m) ↔24in (60cm)

A tap-rooted perennial producing a clump of jaggedly lobed and toothed leaves. Spikes of dandelion-like pink flowerheads are carried on branched stems in summer.

Erigeron 'Charity'
FLEABANE
☼ ◐ 5-9 ↕24in (60cm) ↔18in (45cm)

Leafy clumps of stems produce cheerful, lilac-pink, yellow-centered daisies, singly or in clusters, throughout summer. The flowers are especially popular with bees.

Euphorbia nicaeensis
SPURGE
☼ 5-8 ↕32in (80cm) ↔18in (45cm)

This superb, woody-based plant is valued for its reddish green stems and narrow, blue-bloomy leaves. Green-yellow flowerheads appear in late spring and summer.

Geranium sanguineum 'Max Frei'
BLOODY CRANESBILL
☼ 3-8 ↕8in (20cm) ↔12in (30cm)

The neat, rounded mounds of deeply cut leaves often become richly red-tinted in autumn. A mass of deep magenta flowers appears atop the foliage in summer.

Glaucium flavum
YELLOW HORNED POPPY
☼ 6-9 ↕24in (60cm) ↔18in (45cm)

Mostly found on sand or gravely soil in the wild, this poppy bears bloomy blue-green leaves and stems. Yellow summer flowers are followed by narrow, curved fruits.

Kniphofia 'Atlanta'
RED HOT POKER
☼ ☀ 5-9 ↕4ft (1.2m) ↔30in (75cm)

A magnificent evergreen forming bold clumps of strap-shaped, gray-green leaves. Stout-stemmed orange-red pokers open to yellow flowers in late spring and summer.

OTHER PERENNIALS TOLERANT OF COASTAL EXPOSURE

Achillea tomentosa
Armeria maritima
Artemisia stelleriana
Centranthus ruber, see p.86
Crambe cordifolia, see p.22
Erigeron glaucus
Eryngium spp. and cvs.
Hemerocallis spp. and cvs.
Limonium spp. and cvs.
Yucca filamentosa

Pennisetum alopecuroides 'Hameln'
FOUNTAIN GRASS
☼ 6-9 ↕3ft (1m) ↔4½ft (1.4m)

Bottlebrush-like, greenish white heads of spikelets, borne in summer, age to gray-then golden brown above arching, elegant mounds of grassy leaves.

Papaver orientale 'Cedric Morris'
ORIENTAL POPPY
☼ 2-7 ↕↔36in (90cm)

An exquisite form of a cottage-garden staple forming bold clumps of hairy gray leaves. Its large, frilly-margined, soft pink blooms open from late spring to summer.

Platycodon grandiflorus
BALLOON FLOWER
☼ ☀ 3-8 ↕24in (60cm) ↔12in (30cm)

Large, bell-shaped, purple-blue flowers open from balloonlike, inflated buds in late summer. Blue-green leaves clothe the clumps of erect, branching stems.

Senecio cineraria 'Silver Dust'
SENECIO
☼ 7-9 ↕↔12in (30cm)

Silver-gray felt covers the deeply divided leaves and stems of this striking plant, often grown as an annual. Loose heads of mustard yellow flowers open in summer.

Perennials Tolerant of Exposed, Windy Sites

EXPOSURE TO PERSISTENT or strong winds and heavy rain, particularly in cold areas, can severely damage or stunt the growth of garden plants. Fortunately, a surprisingly large number of hardy perennials will grow and even thrive in such conditions. For best results, protect these perennials with a hedge, shrub border, or other barrier on the windward side.

OTHER PERENNIALS TOLERANT OF EXPOSED, WINDY SITES

Achillea ptarmica
Anchusa azurea
Asclepias tuberosa, see p.104
Astilbe chinensis var. *pumila*
Echinops spp. and cvs.
Eryngium maritimum, see p.120
Limonium spp. and cvs.
Physostegia virginiana
Solidago spp. and cvs.
Viola cornuta, see p.81

Alchemilla conjuncta
LADY'S MANTLE
☼ ☀ 4-8 ↕4in (10cm) ↔20in (50cm)

A tough, creeping perennial providing excellent ground cover with its carpet of attractively fingered leaves, silvery-silky beneath. Green flowers open in summer.

Astrantia major 'Hadspen Blood'
MASTERWORT
☼ ☀ 5-8 ↕18in (45cm) ↔24in (60cm)

Attractive enough with its clumps of long-stalked, deeply lobed and toothed leaves, this masterwort has the added bonus of loose heads of dark red flowers in summer.

Brunnera macrophylla
SIBERIAN BUGLOSS
☼ 3-8 ↕18in (45cm) ↔24in (60cm)

This tough, reliable perennial produces branched heads of bright blue, forget-me-not flowers in spring above bold clumps of heart-shaped, softly-hairy leaves.

Anaphalis margaritacea
PEARLY EVERLASTING
☼ 4-8 ↕↔24in (60cm)

The upright clumps of woolly gray stems bear narrow leaves, white-woolly beneath. Clusters of "everlasting", papery flowers are produced from summer to autumn.

Bergenia × *schmidtii*
BERGENIA
☼ ☀ 4-8 ↕12in (30cm) ↔24in (60cm)

A dependable perennial that bears large clusters of rose-pink flowers in late winter and spring above its handsome mounds of rounded, leathery, rich green leaves.

Centaurea montana f. *alba*
PERENNIAL CORNFLOWER
☼ 3-8 ↕18in (45cm) ↔24in (60cm)

This handsome form of the popular, blue-flowered perennial bears bold, pure white, lacy flowers above clumps of gray-green, leafy stems from late spring into summer.

Euphorbia polychroma
CUSHION SPURGE
☼ ☀ 3-8 ↕16in (40cm) ↔12in (30cm)

An invaluable and utterly reliable plant forming a rounded clump of erect, densely leafy stems that bear long-lasting, greenish yellow flowers from spring into summer.

Leucanthemum x *superbum* 'Wirral Pride'
☼ ☀ 4-8 ↕30in (75cm) ↔24in (60cm)

In summer, this clump-forming perennial bears solitary, large, double white daisy flowers with yellow anemone-type centers on erect stems with dark green leaves.

Polemonium 'Lambrook Mauve'
JACOB'S LADDER
☼ ☀ 3-7 ↕↔18in (45cm)

Erect, branching stems bear loose clusters of bell-shaped, lilac-blue flowers during late spring and early summer above the rounded clumps of deeply divided leaves.

Primula 'Wanda'
PRIMROSE
☼ ☀ 4-8 ↕6in (15cm) ↔8in (20cm)

This vigorous, reliable garden primrose produces its dark, claret red flowers over a long period in spring above compact, low clumps of toothy, purplish green leaves.

Rhodiola rosea
ROSEROOT
☼ 2-8 ↕↔8in (20cm)

Dense heads of tiny, bright yellow flowers top the low clump of fleshy, leafy, blue-green bloomy stems in summer. It is ideal for a rock garden, dry wall, or as edging.

Thermopsis rhombifolia
THERMOPSIS
☼ ☀ 3-8 ↕↔36in (90cm)

In early summer, this creeping perennial bears spires of lupine-like yellow flowers above leaves divided into threes. It forms extensive patches and can be invasive.

Low-allergen Perennials

For people who suffer from asthma, hayfever, or other allergies aggravated by air-borne pollen, gardening and gardens often have to be avoided at certain times of the year, especially during summer. Brushing or touching the foliage or flowers of certain plants can also cause or exacerbate some skin allergies. The following insect-pollinated perennials, however, can usually be relied upon to be non-allergenic, and will allow everyone to enjoy the garden all year round.

Ajuga reptans 'Catlin's Giant'
Bugleweed
3-9 ↕ 6in (15cm) ↔ indefinite

This excellent groundcover produces large, brown-green, semievergreen leaves that age to green. Dark blue flower spikes are borne during late spring and summer.

Aquilegia chrysantha 'Yellow Queen'
Golden Columbine
3-9 ↕ 36in (90cm) ↔ 24in (60cm)

The branched stems of this vigorous, erect perennial bear attractive, divided, ferny leaves and slender-spurred, golden yellow flowers during late spring and summer.

Astilbe 'Irrlicht'
Astilbe
3-9 ↕↔ 20in (50cm)

In late spring and early summer, striking, erect plumes of tiny white flowers top this astilbe's bold clumps of much-divided, dark green leaves. It thrives in moist soil.

Bergenia 'Bressingham White'
Bergenia
3-9 ↕ 18in (45cm) ↔ 24in (60cm)

During spring, fleshy, upright stems freely bear loose clusters of bell-shaped, pure white flowers. The robust clumps of large, leathery leaves are usually evergreen.

Campanula trachelium 'Bernice'
Nettle-leaved Bellflower
5-8 ↕ 30in (75cm) ↔ 12in (30cm)

A beautiful perennial with clumps of erect stems clothed in sharply toothed leaves. It bears axillary, double, bell-shaped, violet-blue summer flowers. May need support.

Digitalis 'Glory of Roundway'
Foxglove
4-8 ↕ 36in (90cm) ↔ 12in (30cm)

This choice hybrid of *D. purpurea* and *D. lutea* has branched, narrow-leaved stems and long racemes of funnel-shaped, pale yellow, pink-tinted flowers in summer.

Geranium psilostemon
Armenian Cranesbill
☼ ☼ 5-8 ↕ 4ft (1.2m) ↔ 36in (90cm)

Fantastic in flower, this striking cranesbill sends up a mound of dense, leafy stems that are covered throughout summer with bright magenta, black-eyed blooms.

Hosta 'Blue Blush'
Hosta
☼ ☼ 3-9 ↕ 8in (20cm) ↔ 16in (40cm)

This striking hostas has clumps of lance-shaped, strongly veined, dark blue-green leaves. It produces stalks of bell-shaped, lavender-blue flowers during summer.

Paeonia 'Duchesse de Nemours'
Peony
☼ ☼ 3-8 ↕↔ 32in (80cm)

The large, fragrant, double white flowers of this strong-growing peony have yellow-based inner petals. Flushed green in bud, the blooms open in early summer.

Penstemon 'Andenken an Friedrich Hahn'
☼ ☼ 6-9 ↕ 30in (75cm) ↔ 24in (60cm)

Also known as *P.* 'Garnet', this is probably the most reliable perennial penstemon. Its deep red flowers are produced on strong, leafy stems from midsummer onward.

Sidalcea 'Oberon'
Checkerbloom
☼ 5-8 ↕ 4ft (1.2m) ↔ 18in (45cm)

During summer, loose racemes of clear rose-pink, hollyhock-like flowers appear on erect, leafy stems. The stem leaves are deeply lobed, the basal ones less so.

Veronica spicata subsp. *incana*
Spike Speedwell
☼ 3-8 ↕ 24in (60cm) ↔ 18in (45cm)

Showy, dense spikes of tiny purple-blue flowers, borne during summer, provide striking contrast with the densely silver-hairy stems and mat of silvery foliage.

Other Low-allergen Perennials

- *Allium* spp. and cvs.
- *Aruncus dioicus*, see p.18
- *Astilbe* spp. and cvs.
- *Dicentra* spp. and cvs.
- *Epimedium* spp. and cvs.
- *Hemerocallis* spp. and cvs.
- *Hosta* spp. and cvs.
- *Iris sibirica* and cvs.
- *Polemonium* spp. and cvs.
- *Solidago* spp. and cvs.

Viola cornuta
Horned Violet
☼ ☼ 6-9 ↕ 6in (15cm) ↔ 16in (40cm)

An excellent and reliable small perennial with a low-spreading, slightly bushy habit. Lightly scented, lilac-blue to violet flowers appear in late spring and summer.

Slug-proof Perennials

Slugs and snails have a voracious appetite when they discover a tasty plant, but what they devour in one garden they may only nibble at in another. Some plants, including many hostas, are always a gourmet treat for slugs and snails and are readily consumed. Others, especially those that have hard-textured, hairy, or poisonous leaves, are often relatively ignored. Here is a selection of the most reliably slug- and snail-proof perennials for the garden.

Allium 'Globemaster'
Ornamental Onion
☼ 4-8 ↕32in (80cm) ↔12in (30cm)

Magnificent for group plantings, this bulb has arching, strap-shaped leaves and huge heads of deep violet flowers in summer. It is loved by both butterflies and bees.

Other Slug-proof Perennials

Achillea spp. and cvs.
Aconitum carmichaelii
Anemone vitifolia
Artemisia spp. and cvs.
Campanula persicifolia
Dicentra eximia
Epimedium spp. and cvs.
Euphorbia spp. and cvs.
Helleborus spp. and cvs.
Heuchera spp. and cvs.
Stachys byzantina, see p.45

Aster ericoides 'Esther'
Heath Aster
☼ 5-8 ↕28in (70cm) ↔12in (30cm)

Bushy clumps of leafy, slender-branched stems are topped by broad heads of small pink, yellow-eyed daisies in late summer and autumn. Useful for its late flowering.

Bergenia 'Silberlicht'
Bergenia
☼ ☀ 3-8 ↕12in (40cm) ↔12in (30cm)

Fleshy, shining, semievergreen leaves form a basal mound. Upright, fleshy stems bear loose clusters of white flowers, aging to pink, above the foliage in spring.

Corydalis lutea
Yellow Corydalis
☼ ☀ 5-8 ↕14in (35cm) ↔12in (30cm)

Slender racemes of tubular yellow flowers are produced continually from late spring to early autumn above mounds of fern-like, semievergreen leaves. It will reseed.

Galanthus 'Atkinsii'
Snowdrop
☀ 3-9 ↕8in (20cm) ↔3in (8cm)

Ideal for naturalizing, this strong-growing bulb has narrow, fleshy, blue-green leaves. In late winter, erect stems carry pendent, pure white flowers with green markings.

Geranium macrorrhizum
WILD CRANESBILL
☼ ☀ 3-8 ↕ 20in (50cm) ↔ 24in (60cm)

An adaptable and reliable, semievergreen carpeter with lobed, aromatic leaves often coloring well in autumn. Clusters of pink to purple flowers appear in early summer.

Helleborus x *nigercors*
HELLEBORE
☀ 6-8 ↕ 12in (30cm) ↔ 36in (90cm)

Welcome clusters of saucer-shaped, white or pink-tinted flowers open from winter to spring above the basal clump of divided, coarse-toothed, evergreen leaves.

Hosta 'Halcyon'
HOSTA
☼ ☀ 3-8 ↕↔ 28in (70cm)

One of the best slug-proof hostas forming bold clumps of attractive, heart-shaped, bluish gray leaves. In summer, pendent, bell-shaped, lavender-blue flowers appear.

Iris chrysographes
IRIS
☼ 2-9 ↕↔ 20in (50cm)

This iris forms handsome, erect clumps of narrow, sword-shaped, gray-green leaves. Stems of fragrant, velvety, reddish purple flowers appear during summer.

Pulmonaria angustifolia subsp. *azurea*
BLUE LUNGWORT
☼ ☀ 2-8 ↕ 10in (25cm) ↔ 18in (45cm)

An attractive lungwort developing a low clump of bristly, unmarked green leaves. In spring, it bears nodding clusters of rich gentian-blue, tubular flowers, red in bud.

Rudbeckia hirta
BLACK-EYED SUSAN
☼ ☀ 3-7 ↕ 30in (80cm) ↔ 36in (90cm)

If kept moist during summer, this cheery biennial or short-lived perennial will bear a succession of dark-eyed yellow daisies in summer and autumn.

Sedum spectabile 'Iceberg'
SHOWY STONECROP
☼ 3-9 ↕↔ 18in (45cm)

Reliable and easy to grow, with mounds of gray-green leaves and fleshy stems topped by flattened heads of white flowers from summer to autumn. Loved by butterflies.

Rabbit-proof Perennials

RABBITS CAN BE A MASSIVE SOURCE of plant damage and loss in the garden, especially in country areas or those close to large, open spaces. Although deer are undoubtedly the more serious pest, rabbits can eat their way through a bed or border faster than any slug or snail. Various methods are recommended for their control, but it does no harm to grow some perennials that rabbits find unpalatable or uninteresting.

Agapanthus 'Blue Giant'
AFRICAN LILY
☼ 7-11 ↕36in (90cm) ↔24in (60cm)

During late summer and early autumn, stout stems bearing large, loose heads of rich blue flowers rise above the bold clump of long, strap-shaped green leaves.

Alchemilla mollis
LADY'S-MANTLE
☼ ◐ 3-8 ↕↔14in (35cm)

This adaptable, reliable plant has mounds of downy, scalloped and lobed, gray-green leaves topped by yellowish green flower clusters during summer. It will self-seed.

Aster ericoides 'Golden Spray'
HEATH ASTER
☼ 3-8 ↕36in (90cm) ↔12in (30cm)

From late summer into autumn, branched heads of small white, pink-tinted daisies with rich yellow centers are produced on a bushy clump of erect, leafy stems.

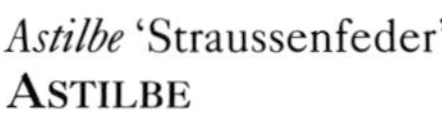

Astilbe 'Straussenfeder'
ASTILBE
☼ ◐ 3-9 ↕36in (90cm) ↔24in (60cm)

Also known as 'Ostrich Plume', which neatly describes the arching sprays of pink flowers in summer and autumn. Its young leaves are attractively bronze-tinted.

Bergenia stracheyi
BERGENIA
☼ 4-8 ↕8in (20cm) ↔12in (30cm)

During early spring, the low mound of leathery, semievergreen leaves is crowned by dense clusters of fragrant, bell-shaped pink flowers. It makes a fine groundcover.

Euphorbia griffithii 'Fireglow'
GRIFFITH'S SPURGE
☼ ◐ 4-8 ↕30in (75cm) ↔36in (90cm)

A vigorous, creeping perennial eventually forming large patches of leafy stems that color richly in autumn. Terminal clusters of fiery orange flowers emerge in summer.

Helleborus × *hybridus*
LENTEN ROSE
◐ 4-9 ↕↔18in (45cm)

A beautiful and sought-after group of hybrids bearing semievergeen leaves and large, nodding, saucer-shaped flowers in a range of colors from late winter to spring.

Lamium maculatum 'Beacon Silver'
SPOTTED LAMIUM
3-8 ↕8in (20cm) ↔3ft (1m)

An excellent groundcover forming carpets of toothed, silvery, green-margined, semi-evergreen leaves. Clusters of pretty, pale pink flowers are produced during summer.

OTHER RABBIT-PROOF PERENNIALS

- *Aconitum* spp. and cvs.
- *Anemone* x *hybrida* and cvs.
- *Aquilegia* x *hybrida* and cvs.
- *Aster novi-belgii* and cvs.
- *Convallaria majalis*
- *Crocosmia* spp. and cvs.
- *Kniphofia* spp. and cvs.
- *Nepeta* x *faassenii*
- *Pulmonaria saccharata* and cvs.
- *Sedum* spp. and cvs.
- *Tradescantia* x *andersoniana*

Paeonia officinalis 'Rubra Plena'
PEONY
3-8 ↕30in (75cm) ↔36in (90cm)

The reliable, old-fashioned, double red peony of cottage gardens. It has clumps of glossy green leaves and bears red blooms with ruffled petals in early summer.

Narcissus 'Mount Hood'
DAFFODIL
3-8 ↕18in (45cm) ↔20in (50cm)

A classic large-flowered trumpet daffodil producing gorgeous white flowers with cream-colored trumpets during spring. It is excellent for planting in groups.

Trollius x *cultorum* 'Earliest of All'
GLOBEFLOWER
3-6 ↕20in (50cm) ↔16in (40cm)

Not the first, but still an early perennial, forming loose clumps of deeply cut leaves. Branched stems bear globular, clear yellow flowers in spring. It prefers heavy soils.

Veratrum album
FALSE HELLEBORE
5-9 ↕6ft (2m) ↔24in (60cm)

Worth growing for its large, handsomely pleated leaves alone, this bold perennial is impressive in groups. The tall plumes of white flowers in summer are a bonus.

Deer-proof Perennials

WITHOUT A DOUBT the most destructive garden visitors of all are deer. Increasingly, deer have become a major problem for gardeners in suburban areas as well as rural and wooded areas. To find a favorite plant demolished after an evening or early morning browsing can be demoralizing. The answer, other than erecting fences or providing deterrents, is to grow at least some perennials that deer are known to find uninteresting or, better still, unpalatable.

Aconitum lycoctonum subsp. *vulparia*
WOLFSBANE
☼ ☀ 5-8 ↕ 5ft (1.5m) ↔ 36in (90cm)

This handsome perennial has finely cut, glossy green foliage and produces straw yellow flowers in summer. Its roots were once used in parts of Europe as wolf bait.

Artemisia ludoviciana 'Silver Queen'
WHITE SAGE
☼ 3-9 ↕↔ 30in (75cm)

A clump-forming, but creeping, perennial worth growing for its lance-shaped, silver-white leaves and heads of woolly white flowers that appear from summer onward.

Astilbe 'Deutschland'
ASTILBE
☼ ☀ 3-9 ↕ 20in (50cm) ↔ 12in (30cm)

In summer, erect panicles of white flowers top the bright, glossy green mound of deeply divided leaves. Good for cutting, it needs some moisture in summer to excel.

OTHER DEER-PROOF PERENNIALS

Achillea spp. and cvs.
Aconitum napellus
Allium spp. and cvs.
Amsonia tabernaemontana
Anemone spp. and cvs.
Aster novi-belgii
Bergenia spp. and cvs.
Cimicifuga spp. and cvs.
Dictamnus albus, see p.108
Epimedium spp. and cvs.
Geranium sanguineum
Helleborus spp. and cvs.
Iris foetidissima
Lamium maculatum
Lavandula angustifolia
Paeonia spp. and cvs.
Rudbeckia fulgida
Santolina chamaecyparissus
Stachys byzantina, see p.45

Centranthus ruber
RED VALERIAN
☼ 4-8 ↕ 36in (90cm) ↔ 24in (60cm)

This woody-based plant has bold clumps of leafy, gray-green stems and fragrant, pink, red, or white flowers in spring and early summer. It thrives in alkaline soil.

Digitalis purpurea Excelsior Hybrids
FOXGLOVE
☀ 4-8 ↕ 6ft (2m) ↔ 24in (60cm)

A bold and colorful short-lived perennial or biennial with a rosette of hairy foliage. Tall, erect spires of funnel-shaped flowers in pastel shades emerge in early summer.

Geranium macrorrhizum 'Bevan's Variety'

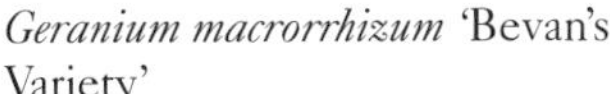

☼ ☀ 3-8 ↕ 20in (50cm) ↔ 24in (60cm)

An excellent, all-round, semievergreen plant, especially useful as groundcover. It flowers in early summer and has aromatic leaves that often color well in autumn.

Iris orientalis
IRIS

☼ 6-9 ↕↔ 36in (90cm)

This robust perennial forms erect clumps or patches of strap-shaped leaves. In early summer, stiff stems carry a succession of attractive white, yellow-stained flowers.

Lysimachia clethroides
LOOSESTRIFE

☼ ☀ 3-8 ↕ 36in (90cm) ↔ 24in (60cm)

A vigorous, fast-spreading perennial that forms a clump of erect, narrowly leafy stems. Its characteristic swan-neck spikes of white flowers are borne in summer.

Narcissus 'Spellbinder'
DAFFODIL

☼ ☀ 3-8 ↕↔ 20in (50cm)

This strong-growing daffodil is especially impressive when planted in bold drifts. The spring flowers are sulphur yellow and have coronas that fade to white with age.

Papaver orientale 'Beauty of Livermere'

☼ 2-7 ↕↔ 36in (90cm)

In early summer, erect, hairy stems bear pale salmon-pink flowers with basal black marks. Clumps of deeply cut, hairy leaves disappear after the flowers fade.

x *Solidaster luteus* 'Lemore'
SOLIDASTER

☼ 5-9 ↕↔ 32in (80cm)

Dense clumps of erect stems clothed in narrow leaves sport sparsely branched heads of pale lemon yellow flowers from summer to autumn. It is good for cutting.

FLORAL EFFECT

△ SUMMER BLOOMS *Mixed colors and flower forms are the strength of this scree planting, which flanks an informal path.*

THE GREATEST ATTRIBUTE of many perennials, flowers can be relied upon to bring fragrance and color to any situation in the garden or home. With blooms in all shades and shapes, in some cases borne over several months, there is scope for imaginative combinations, and for flowers all year round.

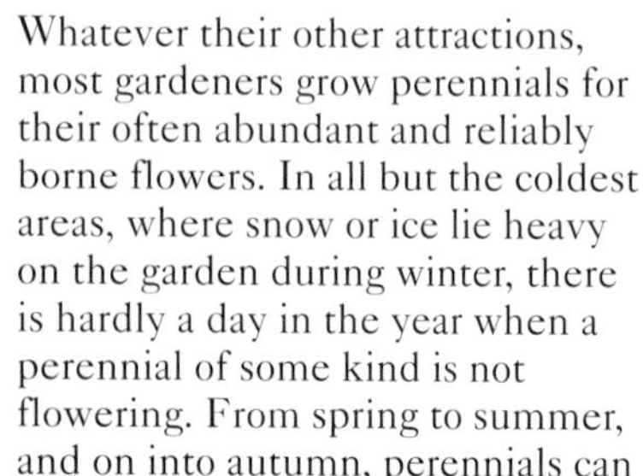

Anemone hupehensis 'September Charm' for autumn flowers

Whatever their other attractions, most gardeners grow perennials for their often abundant and reliably borne flowers. In all but the coldest areas, where snow or ice lie heavy on the garden during winter, there is hardly a day in the year when a perennial of some kind is not flowering. From spring to summer, and on into autumn, perennials can provide gardens with an unbroken, colorful and fragrant display. From late winter into early spring, there is a small but reliable fraternity of perennials that will produce flowers despite the often poor light and intimidating cold.

FLOWER COLOR

With flowers ranging from white and subtle pastel shades to strident reds and golden yellows, perennials will bring a truly formidable range of colors to the garden. These colors can be used to create varied effects, depending on whether you choose to mix them in a natural arrangement, or match them as part of a more structured theme. The strong color contrasts often seen in the wild, where perennials such as goldenrod (*Solidago*) and violet-blue native asters grow together, can inspire garden plantings either using the same or similar plants. To evoke a particular mood, a selection of perennials with similarly toned blooms, whether hot, cool, or pale in color, can be grown together. For a more formal design, themed borders using only one flower color are also an option.

FORM AND STRUCTURE

Flowerheads make an important, if temporary, contribution to the form and structure of a garden landscape. Varying from the statuesque to the fragile, the spheres, plumes, sprays, tall spikes, or flattened flowerheads of perennials can be combined for eye-catching contrast and effect.

△ HOT COLORS *A fiery display of* Hemerocallis *'Stafford' and* Lilium *'Enchantment' brings warmth to a border.*

◁ STRONG CONTRAST *Striking effects can be achieved by using a few contrasting colors, here mainly blue and yellow.*

▷ INFORMAL BEAUTY *Pale Oriental poppies, foxgloves, and* Dictamnus *make a delightful study in height and color.*

Perennials with Spring Flowers

NO GARDEN PERENNIALS are more eagerly awaited than those that flower in spring. This is especially true in cold climates, where there is often little color in the garden to relieve the long, bleak winters. With the increasing warmth and daylight of spring, the garden is rejuvenated as a wealth of perennials, including many bulbs, burst into flower.

Bergenia 'Sunningdale'
BERGENIA
☼ ☀ 3-8 ↕18in (45cm) ↔24in (60cm)

The clumps of leathery, semievergreen leaves turn a warm copper red in winter. Spring brings loose clusters of bell-shaped, lilac-magenta flowers on red stems.

Chionodoxa luciliae
GLORY-OF-THE-SNOW
☼ 3-9 ↕6in (15cm) ↔4in (10cm)

One of the loveliest and most reliable of early spring bulbs, with loose clusters of starry, sky blue, white-eyed flowers. It is particularly impressive planted in drifts.

Hylomecon japonica
HYLOMECON
☀ ☀ 5-8 ↕↔12in (30cm)

This charming poppy relative is excellent in shade, especially as a groundcover. It has deeply divided, toothed leaves and bears its simple flowers into early summer.

SPRING-FLOWERING EVERGREEN TO SEMIEVERGREEN PERENNIALS

Aurinia saxatilis
Epimedium pinnatum subsp. *colchicum*, see p.46
Erysimum 'Bowles' Mauve'
Fragaria vesca
Helleborus argutifolius, see p.114
Helleborus foetidus
Iberis sempervirens
Mitchella repens
Muscari armeniacum

Boykinia jamesii
BOYKINIA
☀ 4-8 PH ↕↔6in (15cm)

A choice perennial bearing loose, upright sprays of frilled, bell-shaped, pinkish red, green-centered flowers above mounds of rounded or kidney-shaped leaves.

Doronicum orientale 'Frühlingspracht'
LEOPARD'S BANE
☼ ☀ 3-8 ↕16in (40cm) ↔36in (90cm)

This colorful plant, also sold as 'Spring Beauty', bears double, golden flowerheads above clumps of scalloped, heart-shaped leaves, which disappear during summer.

Lathyrus vernus 'Alboroseus'
SPRING VETCHLING
☼ ☀ 5-9 ↕16in (40cm) ↔18in (45cm)

The crowded, erect stems of this clump-former produce deeply divided leaves and loose, one-sided racemes of pea-shaped, pink and white flowers. Good with bulbs.

Primula denticulata var. *alba*
DRUMSTICK PRIMROSE
☼ ☀ 3-8 ↕↔ 18in (45cm)

This is the white form of a popular and easily grown perennial. Its rounded heads of yellow-eyed flowers are carried on stout stems above leafy foliage rosettes.

Leucojum vernum var. *carpathicum*
SPRING SNOWFLAKE
☼ ☀ 4-9 ↕ 10in (25cm) ↔ 6in (15cm)

Charming for group plantings, this bulb has tufts of strap-shaped leaves and fleshy stems bearing nodding, bell-shaped white flowers with yellow-tipped segments.

Pulmonaria 'Mawson's Blue'
PULMONARIA
☼ ☀ 4-7 ↕ 14in (35cm) ↔ 18in (45cm)

Low clumps of softly-hairy leaves and clusters of dark blue flowers appear from late winter to spring. A pretty alternative to pulmonarias with spotted leaves.

Narcissus 'King Alfred'
DAFFODIL
☼ ☀ 4-9 ↕ 18in (45cm) ↔ 12in (30cm)

Spectacular in large groups or drifts, this classic daffodil is popular for naturalizing. Strong stems carry large, trumpet-shaped, golden yellow flowers in early spring.

Narcissus 'Thalia'
DAFFODIL
☼ ☀ 4-9 ↕ 14in (35cm) ↔ 6in (15cm)

One of a group of hybrids of *N. triandrus*, this beautiful daffodil has upright stems, each carrying a pair of nodding, milk-white flowers with yellow-tinged throats.

SPRING-FLOWERING HERBACEOUS PERENNIALS

Adonis vernalis, see p.98
Bergenia ciliata
Brunnera macrophylla, see p.78
Cardamine spp.
Euphorbia polychroma, see p.79
Hacquetia epipactis, see p.37
Pachyphragma macrophyllum
Trillium spp. and cvs.
Trollius x *cultorum* 'Earliest of All', see p.85

Perennials with Flowers from Early to Midsummer

After the initial rush of flowers during spring, the scene is set for the wealth of perennials that flower from early to midsummer. Some even bloom intermittently into early autumn. They include many of our most popular and reliable garden and border plants, as well as others that are perhaps less well known, though equally desirable.

Aconitum 'Ivorine'
Monkshood
☼ ◑ 4-7 ↕↔ 36in (90cm)

A vigorous, bushy perennial with clumps of deeply lobed, jaggedly cut leaves. The branching stems carry dense racemes of hooded ivory flowers in early summer.

Baptisia australis
Blue False Indigo
☼ 3-9 ↕ 5ft (1.5m) ↔ 36in (90cm)

Long racemes of blue, white-marked pea-shaped flowers borne in early summer are followed by inflated seed pods. The three-parted leaves are a bloomy blue-green.

Small Perennials with Early/Midsummer Blooms

Astrantia major
Campanula carpatica
Coreopsis verticillata and cvs.
Digitalis grandiflora
Geranium spp. and cvs.
Helianthemum spp. and cvs.
Heuchera sanguinea and cvs.
Incarvillea delavayi, see p.118
Oenothera spp. and cvs.
Platycodon grandiflorus, see p.77

Buphthalmum salicifolium
Buphthalmum
☼ ◑ 4-9 ↕ 24in (60cm) ↔ 18in (45cm)

Yellow daisylike flowers, good for cutting, are borne continuously in summer. The clumps of upright stems are clothed with narrow, willowlike, dark geen leaves.

Delphinium 'Fanfare'
Delphinium
☼ 3-7 ↕ 7ft (2.2m) ↔ 18in (45cm)

Tall and beautiful, this impressive plant bears deeply cut, lobed leaves and dense, branched racemes of semidouble, white-eyed, silver-mauve summer flowers.

Geranium 'Johnson's Blue'
CRANESBILL
☼ ☀ 4-8 ↕18in (45cm) ↔24in (60cm)

One of the best garden cranesbills, this forms a clump of long-stalked, deeply cut leaves. Lavender-blue flowers with pale blue or pink eyes open freely in summer.

Gypsophila paniculata 'Bristol Fairy'
☼ 3-9 ↕↔3½ft (1.1m)

This popular perennial produces a loose mound of slender, branched stems, narrow leaves, and clouds of small, double white summer flowers. Excellent for cut flowers.

Hemerocallis middendorffii
MIDDENDORFF DAYLILY
☼ 3-9 ↕36in (90cm) ↔18in (45cm)

Fragrant, deep orange-yellow flowers open from reddish brown buds in early summer above the bold clumps of arching, strap-shaped leaves. Reblooms during summer.

Iris 'Blue-eyed Brunette'
BEARDED IRIS
☼ ☀ 3-8 ↕36in (90cm) ↔24in (60cm)

The typical fans of sword-shaped, grayish green leaves are topped in early summer by striking, large, reddish brown flowers with lilac splashes and golden beards.

MEDIUM TO TALL PERENNIALS WITH EARLY/MIDSUMMER BLOOMS

Aruncus dioicus, see p.18
Campanula persicifolia
Cimicifuga racemosa
Crambe cordifolia, see p.22
Dictamnus albus, see p.108
Euphorbia griffithii 'Fireglow', see p.84
Geranium psilostemon, see p.81
Heliopsis helianthoides and cvs.
Hemerocallis spp. and cvs.
Iris sibirica

Malva alcea var. *fastigiata*
MALLOW
☼ 4-8 ↕32in (80cm) ↔24in (60cm)

The continuous display of hollyhock-like, five-petaled, deep pink flowers often lasts into autumn. Finely divided leaves clothe the narrow clumps of upright stems.

Scabiosa caucasica 'Clive Greaves'
SCABIOUS
☼ 3-7 ↕↔24in (60cm)

This long-blooming perennial is always reliable in its flowering. The flattened, lavender-blue flowers, good for cutting, are borne from early summer to autumn.

Stachys macrantha
STACHYS
☼ 4-8 ↕24in (60cm) ↔12in (30cm)

From early summer onward, the handsome rosettes of wrinkled and scalloped, heart-shaped leaves are topped by spikes of long-tubed, pink-purple flowers.

Perennials with Flowers from Mid- to Late Summer

MANY OF THE PERENNIALS that flower in the middle of summer do so over a long period, taking advantage of the available warmth and sunlight. The following selection includes some plants that begin flowering in early summer and others that continue blooming into early autumn, earning their place in the garden by extending the period of interest.

Aster amellus 'Veilchenkönigin'
ITALIAN ASTER
☼ 5-8 ↕ 20in (50cm) ↔ 18in (45cm)

An excellent late summer perennial with clumps of erect, leafy stems topped by broad, flattened clusters of bright yellow-centered, violet-purple daisy flowers.

Coreopsis grandiflora 'Badengold'
LARGE-FLOWERED TICKSEED
☼ ☀ 4-9 ↕ 36in (90cm) ↔ 18in (45cm)

This bright, cheerful-looking perennial has finely divided leaves and clumps of slim, erect stems bearing orange-centered, deep yellow daisies throughout summer.

Digitalis x *mertonensis*
STRAWBERRY FOXGLOVE
☼ ☀ 3-8 ↕ 36in (90cm) ↔ 12in (30cm)

A robust, clump-forming plant bearing tall, upright spikes of tubular, strawberry pink, rose, or white summer flowers. Its veiny leaves are also attractive.

Inula ensifolia
SWORD-LEAVED INULA
☼ ☀ 4-9 ↕ 24in (60cm) ↔ 12in (30cm)

A thoroughly reliable perennial producing narrow leaves and dense, bushy clumps of erect stems. These carry golden yellow daisies over a long period in late summer.

Kniphofia 'Samuel's Sensation'
TORCH LILY
☼ ☀ 5-9 ↕ 5ft (1.5m) ↔ 30in (75cm)

From late summer to early autumn, the bold clumps of long, strap-shaped leaves are dwarfed by stiff-stemmed heads of bright scarlet flowers, aging to yellow.

OTHER PERENNIALS WITH FLOWERS IN MIDSUMMER

Allium senescens
Aster x *frikartii*
Campanula poscharskyana
Ceratostigma plumbaginoides, see p.44
Crocosmia 'Lucifer', see p.116
Hemerocallis spp. and cvs.
Tanacetum parthenium
Tricyrtis hirta
Veronica austriaca subsp. *teucrium* 'Crater Lake Blue'

Lavatera 'Rosea'
MALLOW
☼ 8-10 ↕↔ 6ft (2m)

A popular and reliable mallow for warm-climate gardens that forms a large, woody-based, semievergreen bush covered with deep pink flowers during summer.

OTHER PERENNIALS WITH FLOWERS IN LATE SUMMER

Aconitum x *cammarum* 'Bicolor', see p.18
Aster novae-angliae
Begonia grandis
Boltonia asteroides
Gentiana asclepiadea, see p.107
Helenium 'Septemberfuchs', see p.104

Monarda 'Prärienacht'
BEE BALM
☼ ☀ 4-8 ↕ 36in (90cm) ↔ 24in (60cm)

The dense clumps of downy, four-angled stems bear crowded heads of purple-lilac flowers with red-tinted green bracts. All parts are aromatic when bruised.

Nepeta sibirica
CATMINT
☼ ☀ 3-7 ↕ 36in (90cm) ↔ 18in (45cm)

Aromatic, toothy leaves clothe the erect clumps of four-angled stems. The long, interrupted spikes of large, deep violet to lilac-blue flowers are loved by bees.

Physostegia virginiana 'Vivid'
OBEDIENT PLANT
☼ ☀ 3-9 ↕ 24in (60m) ↔ 12in (30cm)

During summer, spikes of bright purple-pink flowers, excellent for cutting, top the dense clumps of smooth, four-angled, erect stems clothed in narrow leaves.

Salvia x *sylvestris* 'Mainacht'
☼ 5-9 ↕ 24in (60cm) ↔ 12in (30cm)

In English, its name, 'May Night', aptly describes the velvety, dark indigo-blue flowers with purple bracts that are borne in long spikes on leafy, four-angled stems.

Verbena bonariensis
VERBENA
☼ 7-9 ↕ 6ft (2m) ↔ 18in (45cm)

Bees and butterflies are both attracted to the clusters of tiny lilac-purple flowers that crown the tall, branching stems. It is often grown as an annual. Seeds freely.

Perennials with Autumn Flowers

FOR MANY GARDENERS, especially in cool temperate zones, autumn is dominated by the brilliant tints of dying leaves and the equally colorful effect of seedheads, berries, and other fruits. Comparatively few perennials choose to flower at this time, but those that do are all the more valued, as their late displays enliven the garden before the onset of winter.

Cyclamen hederifolium
HARDY CYCLAMEN
5-9 ↕4in (10cm) ↔6in (15cm)

Neatly lobed, beautifully marbled leaves follow the exquisite, slender-stalked, pink or white flowers. Useful as a groundcover under trees or for group plantings.

Aconitum carmichaelii 'Arendsii'
MONKSHOOD
3-9 ↕4ft (1.2m) ↔24in (60cm)

A bold, clump-forming perennial valued for its stems of dense, deeply cut, dark green leaves and panicles of helmeted, purple-blue, dark-eyed flowers.

Cimicifuga simplex 'Elstead'
KAMCHATKA BUGBANE
3-8 ↕4ft (1.2m) ↔24in (60cm)

The tall, arching stems of this graceful perennial bear long, cylindrical racemes of tiny white flowers above deeply divided, dark green to purple-tinted leaves.

Leucanthemella serotina
MOON DAISY
4-9 ↕6ft (2m) ↔36in (90cm)

Late and lovely, this bold daisy has clumps of tall, leafy stems and sprays of big white blooms that face and follow the sun. Once known as *Chrysanthemum uliginosum*.

Anemone hupehensis 'September Charm'
JAPANESE ANEMONE
5-9 ↕30in (75cm) ↔24in (60cm)

This handsome anemone forms clumps of dark shoots with three-lobed leaflets. It produces a long succession of clear pink flowers from late summer into autumn.

Colchicum 'Waterlily'
AUTUMN CROCUS
4-9 ↕5in (12cm) ↔4in (10cm)

This is one of the most spectacular dwarf bulbs, especially in large drifts. Its double, slender-tubed, pinkish lilac blooms may need support. Leaves emerge in spring.

Nerine bowdenii 'Mark Fenwick'
NERINE
8-10 ↕18in (45cm) ↔12in (30cm)

Spectacular in autumn, this bulb's smooth stems flaunt loose umbels of lilylike pink flowers. The broad, strap-shaped leaves follow later. It is superb in group plantings.

Schizostylis coccinea 'Major'
CRIMSON FLAG
☼ 6-9 ↕24in (60cm) ↔12in (30cm)

This relative of gladiolus bears flattened, sword-shaped leaves and bold spikes of large, satin-textured red flowers. Plant it in groups for a striking effect.

OTHER PERENNIALS WITH AUTUMN FLOWERS

Anemone x *hybrida*
Aster spp. and cvs.
Colchicum spp. and cvs.
Crocus speciosus
Eupatorium spp. and cvs.
Gentiana spp. and cvs.
Kniphofia triangularis, see p.105
Leucojum autumnale
Tricyrtis hirta var. *alba*
Vernonia spp.

Strobilanthes atropurpureus
STROBILANTHES
☼ ☀ 7-9 ↕4ft (1.2m) ↔36in (90cm)

An excellent plant that is not commonly cultivated. The curved, hooded, indigo-blue or purple flowers are borne freely on densely branched, bushy, and leafy stems.

Sedum 'Vera Jameson'
STONECROP
☼ 3-9 ↕10in (25cm) ↔18in (45cm)

A true gem among the autumn-flowering sedums, this has low mounds of bloomy, blue-purple leaves and crowded, rounded heads of star-shaped, rose-pink flowers.

Tricyrtis formosana
TOAD LILY
☀ ☀ 5-9 ↕32in (80cm) ↔18in (45cm)

The curious white flowers, spotted red-purple, of this erect, clump-forming plant deserve a close look to fully appreciate their beauty. The foliage is handsome too.

Vernonia crinita
IRONWEED
☼ ☀ 4-7 ↕6ft (2m) ↔3ft (90cm)

From late summer to autumn, flattened clusters of reddish purple flowerheads top the erect, strong-growing, narrow-leaved stems of this stately, native ironweed.

Perennials with Winter Flowers

IN CLIMATES WHERE winters bring almost all growth to a standstill, the appearance of any plant in flower is always a surprise. However, certain perennials, including many bulbs, bloom during winter or very early spring despite the hostile conditions. Those suggested here will bring much-needed color at a time when other herbaceous plants have died down.

Adonis vernalis
ADONIS
☼ 5-8 ↕15in (38cm) ↔18in (45cm)

In late winter and early spring, cupped, golden yellow flowers top clumps of ferny, bright green leaves. For earliest bloom, plant in a sheltered, south-facing location.

Crocus tommasinianus
CROCUS
☼ ☀ 3-8 ↕4in (10cm) ↔3in (7.5cm)

Easily naturalized, this popular bulb bears slender-tubed, scented, pale silvery lilac to reddish purple flowers in winter and early spring above clumps of narrow leaves.

Eranthis hyemalis
WINTER ACONITE
☼ ☀ 4-9 ↕3in (8cm) ↔2in (5cm)

The cup-shaped, bright yellow flowers of winter aconite are a cheery sight above the ruffs of toothed leaves in winter and early spring. Superb planted in large drifts.

OTHER PERENNIALS WITH WINTER FLOWERS

Adonis amurensis
Bergenia x *schmidtii*, see p.78
Chionodoxa luciliae, see p.90
Crocus chrysanthus
Helleborus argutifolius, see p.114
Helleborus x *hybridus*, see p.84
Iris reticulata
Narcissus 'February Gold'
Pulmonaria spp. and cvs.
Viola odorata

Arisarum vulgare
MONK'S COWL
☼ ☀ 8-9 ↕6in (15cm) ↔5in (13cm)

This curious *Arum* relative bears broadly arrow-shaped green leaves followed by hooded, brown- or purple-striped flowers, each with a protruding "nose".

Cyclamen coum f. *albissimum*
HARDY CYCLAMEN
☼ ☀ 5-9 ↕4in (10cm) ↔6in (15cm)

The low mounds of kidney-shaped, fleshy green or attractively marbled leaves are accompanied in winter and early spring by white flowers with carmine-red mouths.

Galanthus nivalis 'Sandersii'
SNOWDROP
☀ 3-9 ↕↔4in (10cm)

A charming and unusual variation of the familiar snowdrop, in which the flower ovaries and the tips of the inner segments are bright yellow. It is slow to increase.

Galanthus reginae-olgae subsp. *vernalis*
SNOWDROP
☼ 6-9 ↕↔4in (10cm)

Faintly scented, nodding white flowers borne in late winter and spring have inner segments tipped green. It differs from the common snowdrop in its darker leaves.

Iris unguicularis 'Walter Butt'
WINTER IRIS
☼ 7-9 ↕12in (30cm) ↔16in (40cm)

Over many weeks, this beautiful winter-flowering plant produces a succession of large, fragrant, pale lavender-blue flowers from clumps of narrow, evergreen leaves.

Lathraea clandestina
BLUE TOOTHWORT
☼ ☀ 5-9 ↕2in (5cm) ↔12in (30cm)

This parasitic plant can grow on the roots of trees such as alder, willow, and poplar. Two-lipped mauve flowers emerge from the white, scaly clumps during late winter.

Helleborus foetidus 'Wester Flisk'
STINKING HELLEBORE
☼ ☀ 6-9 ↕32in (80cm) ↔18in (45cm)

The stems, fingerlike leaves, and flower-stalks of this evergreen plant are suffused with red. The pendent, bell-shaped, pale green flowers have purple mouths.

Helleborus niger 'Potter's Wheel'
CHRISTMAS ROSE
☀ 3-8 ↕12in (30cm) ↔18in (45cm)

A reliable selection of a favorite cottage-garden perennial producing bowl-shaped white flowers with green eyes above low clumps of leathery, overwintering foliage.

Narcissus 'Bowles' Early Sulphur'
DAFFODIL
☼ ☀ 3-7 ↕8in (20cm) ↔5in (13cm)

Bearing mid-yellow flowers in late winter, this seedling of *N. asturiensis* is one of the earliest-flowering small daffodils. It forms clumps of narrow, strap-shaped leaves.

Perennials with a Long Flowering Season

MOST GARDEN PERENNIALS, especially spring-blooming ones, flower only for a relatively limited period. The invaluable perennials suggested below offer unusually long flowering seasons. They either bloom throughout summer or from summer into autumn. They are especially effective for bringing an element of continuity to the garden.

Astrantia major 'Shaggy'
MASTERWORT
☼ ☀ 5-8 ↕36in (90cm) ↔18in (45cm)

Clusters of tiny flowers surrounded by large, jagged, green-tipped white bracts are borne on branching stems in summer. The deeply cut leaves form bold clumps.

Dicentra 'Stuart Boothman'
DICENTRA
☀ 3-9 ↕12in (30cm) ↔16in (40cm)

A creeping perennial forming clumps of divided, fernlike, blue-gray leaves. Sprays of locket-shaped, pendent, deep pink flowers emerge from spring to summer.

Geranium x *riversleaianum* 'Russell Prichard'
☼ ☀ 6-8 ↕12in (30cm) ↔3ft (1m)

Ideal as a groundcover, this low-grower has trailing stems clothed in neatly lobed, sharply toothed, gray-green leaves. Deep magenta flowers appear during summer.

OTHER PERENNIALS WITH A LONG FLOWERING SEASON

Aster x *frickartii* 'Mönch', see p.16
Campanula carpatica
Coreopsis verticillata 'Moonbeam', see p.108
Corydalis lutea, see p.82
Dicentra eximia and cvs.
Gaura lindheimeri, see p.108
Geranium sanguineum 'Prostratum'
Hemerocallis 'Stella de Oro', see p.16
Viola cornuta, see p.81

Dianthus deltoides
MAIDEN PINK
☼ 3-9 ↕8in (20cm) ↔12in (30cm)

This reliable pink bears dark-eyed, white, pink, or red flowers throughout summer above spreading mats of slender, narrow-leaved stems. Thrives in well-drained soil.

Epilobium glabellum
EPILOBIUM
☼ ☀ 5-8 ↕↔8in (20cm)

Clumps of arching stems densely clothed in semievergreen leaves produce creamy white or pink-tinted flowers in summer. It prefers a site in cool, damp shade.

Geum 'Red Wings'
GEUM
☼ ☀ 4-7 ↕24in (60cm) ↔16in (40cm)

Flowering freely throughout summer, this perennial produces semidouble, brilliant scarlet flowers on branched stems above clumps of softly-hairy, fresh green foliage.

Oenothera macrocarpa
OZARK SUNDROPS
☼ 4-8 ↕6in (15cm) ↔20in (50cm)

Better known as *O. missouriensis*, this vigorous plant has prostrate stems, willowy leaves, and a succession of golden yellow flowers from late spring into autumn.

Phygelius x *rectus* 'African Queen'
CAPE FIGWORT
☼ 8-9 ↕3ft (1m) ↔4½ft (1.4m)

A free-flowering plant with loose clumps of four-angled, woody-based stems. The pendent, tubular, pale red flowers, borne in summer, have yellow mouths.

Salvia microphylla
SAGE
☼ ◐ 10-11 ↕↔4ft (1.2m)

The softly-hairy, evergreen leaves of this woody-based perennial smell of black currants when bruised. Bright red flowers are produced from summer to autumn.

Scabiosa caucasica 'Miss Willmott'
SCABIOUS
☼ 3-7 ↕36in (90cm) ↔24in (60cm)

Large, solitary white flowerheads with creamy white centers adorn the clumps of upright stems in summer. The gray-green stem leaves are deeply divided.

Tradescantia x *andersoniana* 'Isis'
SPIDERWORT
☼ ◐ 3-9 ↕↔20in (50cm)

Dense clumps of upright stems clothed in long, strap-shaped leaves carry clusters of attractive, large, three-petaled, dark blue flowers during summer and autumn.

Viola 'Bowles' Black'
JOHNNY-JUMP-UP
☼ ◐ 3-8 ↕4in (10cm) ↔8in (20cm)

A charming pansy relative with evergreen tufts of leafy stems. It bears a succession of velvety black flowers with golden eyes from spring to autumn. Self-seeds freely.

Perennials with Flowers in Flattened Heads or Sprays

THERE ARE MANY WAYS of creating interest in a border other than using plants of differing heights or varying foliage. One is to plant perennials that branch horizontally, or have flattened flowerheads or flowers borne along the same plane. These will provide a sharp contrast to plants that have an upright or rounded habit, or bear tall spikes of flowers.

Achillea 'Coronation Gold'
YARROW
☼ 3-9 ↕36in (90cm) ↔18in (45cm)

The flattened heads of tiny yellow flowers in summer and autumn are excellent for cutting and drying. Deeply divided, silver-gray leaves form a semievergreen clump.

Chaerophyllum hirsutum 'Roseum'
CHAEROPHYLLUM
☼ ◑ 5-8 ↕24in (60cm) ↔20in (50cm)

Flattened, lilac-pink flowerheads, borne in early summer, create a lacy effect above the clumps of hairy stems covered with ferny, deeply divided leaves.

Aster lateriflorus 'Horizontalis'
CALICO ASTER
☼ ◑ 3-8 ↕24in (60cm) ↔16in (40cm)

This dense, bushy aster has a distinctive horizontal branching habit, small leaves, and tiny pink-mauve flowers in autumn, when the leaves turn coppery purple.

Sambucus ebulus
DWARF ELDERBERRY
☼ ◑ 4-9 ↕36in (90cm) ↔indefinite

A vigorous, suckering perennial with erect stems clothed in deeply divided leaves. The large, sweet-scented white flowers in summer are followed by black berries.

Sedum spectabile
SHOWY STONECROP
☼ 3-8 ↕↔18in (45cm)

This easy-to-grow perennial is adored by butterflies and bees. During late summer, flattened heads of pink flowers cover the low mound of fleshy, grayish leaves.

Selinum wallichianum
SELINUM
☼ ◑ 7-9 ↕4ft (1.2m) ↔24in (60cm)

A lovely member of the carrot family with erect stems and divided, ferny leaves. In summer and autumn, tiny white flowers with black anthers are borne in flat heads.

OTHER PERENNIALS WITH FLAT HEADS OR SPRAYS OF FLOWERS

Achillea filipendulina (see p.70) and cvs.
Aster amellus and cvs.
Ligularia dentata
Phlox stolonifera
Sambucus adnata
Solidago 'Crown of Rays'
Solidago rigida
Tanacetum vulgare
Thalictrum aquilegiifolium
Verbena canadensis

Perennials with Flowers in Spikes

PERENNIALS WITH TALL, SPIKELIKE HEADS of flowers can create bold and dramatic effects, bringing structure and height to garden displays as they rise above other plants in stiff, tight spires or elegant, tapering racemes. In most flower spikes, the blooms open from the base upwards but some, like those of *Liatris* species, open from the top down.

Delphinium 'Butterball'
DELPHINIUM
☼ 3-7 ↕5ft (1.5m) ↔30in (75cm)

In early summer, this gorgeous perennial bears dense, tapered racemes of creamy white, semidouble flowers on sturdy, erect stems clothed in deeply cut leaves.

Digitalis parviflora
RUSTY FOXGLOVE
◑ 7-9 ↕4ft (1.2m) ↔18in (45cm)

Stiff, dense spikes of golden brown, red-veined flowers rise over low, leafy rosettes in summer, creating an effect quite unlike the common foxglove (*D. purpurea*).

Epilobium angustifolium f. *album*
WHITE-FLOWERED FIREWEED
☼ ◑ 3-7 ↕5ft (1.5m) ↔3ft (1m)

The erect stems of this vigorous perennial are clothed in narrow, willowlike leaves and sport long spires of white flowers with green sepals in summer. Self-seeds freely.

Kniphofia 'Erecta'
TORCH LILY
☼ ◑ 6-9 ↕36in (90cm) ↔24in (60cm)

A robust, clump-forming plant with stiff stems and strap-shaped leaves. The dense pokers of coral-red flowers become erect after opening in summer.

Ligularia 'The Rocket'
LIGULARIA
☼ ◑ 4-8 ↕6ft (1.8m) ↔3ft (1m)

Tall, black-stemmed spires of tiny yellow flowers rise impressively in summer above the clumps of long-stalked, heart-shaped, toothy leaves. Best in constantly moist soil.

OTHER PERENNIALS WITH FLOWERS IN SPIKES

Cimicifuga racemosa
Dictamnus albus, see p.108
Digitalis x *mertonensis*, see p.94
Liatris spp. and cvs.
Lobelia cardinalis
Lysimachia punctata, see p.51
Salvia x *superba*
Solidago sempervirens
Veronicastrum virginicum f. *album*, see p.29

Verbascum chaixii 'Album'
NETTLE-LEAVED MULLEIN
☼ 4-8 ↕36in (90cm) ↔18in (45cm)

Striking and reliable, this mullein bears erect, often branched stems crowded with white, mauve-centered flowers in summer over rosettes of hairy, gray-green leaves.

Perennials with Hot, Fiery-colored Flowers

FIERY-COLORED FLOWERS may not appeal to gardeners with delicate tastes, but for many others they inject life and passion into the garden. A single hot-colored perennial, reflecting the intensity and warmth of the sun, can brighten an otherwise bland border. Alternatively, combining a few of them in a mixed planting will create a riot of color.

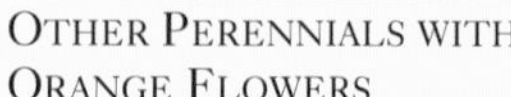
OTHER PERENNIALS WITH ORANGE FLOWERS

Belamcanda chinensis
Euphorbia griffithii 'Fireglow', see p.84
Fritillaria imperialis
Helenium 'Brilliant'
Helianthemum 'Fire Dragon'
Kniphofia 'Pfitzeri'
Lilium 'Enchantment'
Lilium superbum
Phlox paniculata 'Orange Perfection'
Silene virginica

Asclepias tuberosa
BUTTERFLY WEED
☼ 3-9 ↕3ft (90cm) ↔24in (60cm)

Rounded, glowing orange flower clusters crown the erect stems of this sun-loving native wildflower in summer, attracting butterflies. Do not move once established.

Dahlia 'Bishop of Llandaff'
DAHLIA
☼ 7-11 ↕3½ft (1.1m) ↔18in (45cm)

In late summer, the semidouble, glowing red blooms of this popular tender plant are striking against its dusky red leaves. Overwinter the roots indoors in the north.

Geum coccineum
SCARLET AVENS
☼ ☀ 4-7 ↕20in (50cm) ↔12in (30cm)

Throughout spring and summer, slender, branching stems carry orange-red flowers with golden stamens above a loose clump of deeply divided, hairy green leaves.

Crocosmia masoniorum
CROCOSMIA
☼ ☀ 5-9 ↕4ft (1.2m) ↔24in (60cm)

A classic perennial forming bold clumps of sword-shaped, pleated leaves. Arching spikes of trumpet-shaped, rich orange-red flowers in open summer. Good for cutting.

Gaillardia x *grandiflora* 'Dazzler'
BLANKET FLOWER
☼ 4-9 ↕30in (75cm) ↔18in (45cm)

This bushy, often short-lived perennial has big, daisy flowerheads in summer and early autumn. The orange-red blooms are yellow-tipped with maroon centers.

Helenium 'Septemberfuchs'
HELENIUM
☼ 3-7 ↕5ft (1.5m) ↔24in (60cm)

In late summer and autumn, stout clumps of upright, leafy stems carry a multitude of brilliant orange-brown, yellow-suffused daisy flowers with brown hearts.

Hemerocallis fulva 'Flore Pleno'
DAYLILY
☼ ☀ 2-9 ↕30in (75cm) ↔4ft (1.2m)

In summer, erect stems bearing trumpet-shaped, double, orange-brown flowers with dark red centers rise above the bold clump of strap-shaped, arching leaves.

Kniphofia triangularis
RED HOT POKER
☼ 6-9 ↕30in (75cm) ↔18in (45cm)

This species is late-flowering and reliable. It forms a clump of slender, grassy leaves and produces dramatic spikes of reddish orange flowers during autumn.

Lychnis chalcedonica 'Flore Pleno'
MALTESE CROSS
☼ 3-9 ↕4ft (1.2m) ↔18in (45cm)

During summer, erect, hairy, leafy stems carry dense clusters of double scarlet flowers. It may need support. The single-flowered form is also very attractive.

Monarda 'Squaw'
BEE BALM
☼ 4-8 ↕36in (90cm) ↔18in (45cm)

In summer and autumn, bold clumps of hairy stems carry dense clusters of bright red flowers loved by bees and humming-birds. Leaves are aromatic when bruised.

Potentilla 'Monsieur Rouillard'
POTENTILLA
☼ 5-9 ↕18in (45cm) ↔24in (60cm)

This potentilla has a loose clump of erect or spreading stems with deeply divided leaves. Its double, deep blood red flowers with yellow markings open in summer.

Primula 'Inverewe'
CANDELABRA PRIMROSE
☼ ☀ 6-8 ↕↔30in (75cm)

A strong-growing, semievergreen primrose for damp sites with a rosette of toothed leaves. Mealy-white stems carry whorls of striking, bright red flowers in summer.

OTHER PERENNIALS WITH RED FLOWERS

Achillea 'Fanal'
Crocosmia 'Lucifer', see p.116
Hemerocallis 'Pardon Me'
Heuchera 'Mt. Saint Helens'
Hibiscus moscheutos 'Lord Baltimore'
Lilium canadense
Lobelia cardinalis
Monarda didyma 'Gardenview Scarlet'
Papaver orientale 'Glowing Embers'
Potentilla 'Gibson's Scarlet', see p.75

Perennials with Cool-colored Flowers

PINK, BLUE, AND PALE YELLOW are all colors that are cool to the eye. They bring a delicate subtlety to plantings in the garden. White too, plays a similar role. When used with care and discretion, these cool-colored flowers can achieve a soothing effect at any season, but especially if they bloom during the heat of summer.

Agapanthus 'Snowy Owl'
AFRICAN LILY
☼ ◐ 8-10 ↕4ft (1.2m) ↔24in (60cm)

Sturdy stems carry large, loosely rounded umbels of bell-shaped, pure white flowers in late summer above the bold clumps of narrow, strap-shaped green leaves.

Astilbe 'Venus'
ASTILBE
☼ ◐ 3-9 ↕36in (90cm) ↔18in (45cm)

Large, frothy, conical plumes of tiny pink flowers rise above robust clumps of much-divided, bright green, handsome leaves in early summer. It prefers a moist soil.

Centaurea pulcherrima
CENTAUREA
☼ 4-8 ↕16in (40cm) ↔24in (60cm)

Slender stems rise from clumps of deeply lobed or entire, woolly-backed leaves to bear lovely rose-pink, pale-centered flowers from late spring to early summer.

OTHER PERENNIALS WITH EARLY, COOL-COLORED FLOWERS

Anemone nemorosa
Brunnera macrophylla, see p.78
Corydalis flexuosa 'China Blue', see p.65
Dicentra spectabilis 'Alba', see p.108
Epimedium grandiflorum 'Rose Queen', see p.148
Heuchera 'Chatter Box'
Phlox divaricata
Polemonium caeruleum
Thalictrum aquilegiifolium

Anchusa azurea 'Loddon Royalist'
ITALIAN BUGLOSS
☼ 3-8 ↕36in (90cm) ↔24in (60cm)

The sturdy clumps of erect, leafy, roughly hairy stems sport branched heads of pretty, deep blue flowers, each with a white eye, in early summer. It will self-sow.

Campanula persicifolia 'Telham Beauty'
☼ ◐ 3-7 ↕36in (90cm) ↔12in (30cm)

A lovely form of a popular cottage-garden perennial with racemes of large, light blue, bell-shaped flowers on tall, slender stems in summer. Easy to grow and reliable.

Chrysanthemum 'Clara Curtis'
CHRYSANTHEMUM
☼ 4-9 ↕30in (75cm) ↔24in (60cm)

Scented, long-lasting, clear pink daisylike flowers are borne freely from late summer into autumn. Finely-cut leaves cover the bushy clump of stems.

Delphinium 'Blue Bees'
DELPHINIUM
☼ 3-7 ↕ 3ft (1m) ↔ 18in (45cm)

The wiry, upright, branching stems bear deeply cut leaves and racemes of long-spurred, clear blue, white-eyed flowers in early summer and again in late summer.

Gentiana asclepiadea
WILLOW GENTIAN
☼ ◐ 5-7 ↕ 36in (90cm) ↔ 12in (60cm)

Pairs of willowlike leaves clothe the bold clumps of arching stems. Pale or deep blue flowers emerge from the upper leaf axils during late summer and autumn.

Iris winogradowii
IRIS
☼ 7-9 ↕ 3in (7.5cm) ↔ 4in (10cm)

In early spring, primrose yellow flowers with green-flecked falls rise above tufts of four-sided, slender leaves. It is excellent for containers, troughs, or a rock garden.

Monarda 'Croftway Pink'
BEE BALM, BERGAMOT
☼ ◐ 4-8 ↕ 36in (90cm) ↔ 24in (60cm)

Popular with bees, this aromatic perennial has erect stems clothed in paired leaves. In summer, it freely bears clusters of clear rose-pink flowers with dark bracts.

Paeonia 'Sarah Bernhardt'
PEONY
☼ ◐ 3-8 ↕↔ 36in (90cm)

This robust perennial produces clumps of upright, leafy stems that bear very large, fragrant, fully double, rose-pink blooms in early summer. Excellent for cutting.

Penstemon heterophyllus 'Blue Gem'
☼ ◐ 6-9 ↕↔ 16in (40cm)

Striking in flower, this evergreen or semi-evergreen, woody-based perennial bears slender, glossy leaves and dense, erect racemes of tubular blue summer flowers.

OTHER PERENNIALS WITH LATE, COOL-COLORED FLOWERS

Anemone japonica 'Pamina'
Begonia grandis
Boltonia asteroides 'Pink Beauty'
Clematis integrifolia
Geranium × *oxonianum* 'A.T. Johnson'
Liriope muscari, see p.65
Nepeta 'Six Hills Giant', see p.121
Phlox paniculata 'Fujiyama', see p.109
Platycodon grandiflorus f. *albus*

Sidalcea 'Elsie Heugh'
CHECKERBLOOM
☼ 5-8 ↕ 36in (90cm) ↔ 18in (45cm)

A reliable plant with erect or spreading stems that bear deeply lobed stem leaves, and tall racemes of long-lasting, satiny, purple-pink flowers during summer.

Perennials with Pale-colored Flowers

PALE-COLORED FLOWERS provide one of the most effective means of illuminating a dark corner or shaded border in the garden. They shine when set against a backdrop of dark foliage. At the end of the day when darkness is falling, they attract and reflect any available light, drawing attention to borders and beds.

Anthemis tinctoria 'Sauce Hollandaise'
GOLDEN MARGUERITE
3-8 ↕↔ 24in (60cm)

Long-stalked, yellow-centered, pale cream daisy heads are borne freely over many weeks in summer above clumps of finely divided, dark green leaves.

Coreopsis verticillata 'Moonbeam'
THREADLEAF COREOPSIS
3-9 ↕ 20in (50cm) ↔ 18in (45cm)

In summer, a profusion of lemon yellow flowerheads covers this low, bushy plant. Its slender, branched stems bear finely cut leaves. Ideal for the front of a border.

Dictamnus albus
GAS PLANT
3-8 ↕ 36in (90cm) ↔ 24in (60cm)

A slow-growing plant forming clumps of aromatic, deeply divided foliage. In early summer, bold, erect racemes of white flowers with conspicuous stamens appear.

OTHER PERENNIALS WITH PALE-COLORED FLOWERS

Achillea 'Moonshine'
Alcea rugosa
Aquilegia canadensis 'Corbett'
Echinacea purpurea 'White Swan'
Lilium candidum
Oenothera speciosa 'Rosea', see p.21
Phlox carolina 'Miss Lingard'
Platycodon grandiflorus 'Shell Pink'
Polemonium carneum
Potentilla recta var. *pallida*

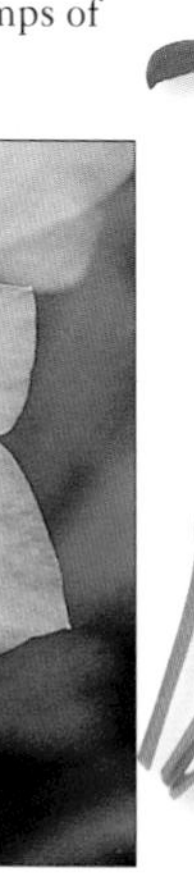

Campanula persicifolia 'Chettle Charm'
PEACH-LEAVED BELLFLOWER
3-7 ↕ 36in (90cm) ↔ 12in (30cm)

One of the loveliest cultivars of a popular perennial with tall slender stems, narrow leaves, and sprays of pale, bell-shaped summer flowers tinged blue at the edges.

Dicentra spectabilis 'Alba'
BLEEDING HEART
2-9 ↕ 24in (30cm) ↔ 18in (45cm)

This beautiful and elegant perennial has ferny, pale green foliage and produces long stems hung with locket-shaped white flowers from late spring to early summer.

Gaura lindheimeri
WHITE GAURA
5-9 ↕ 4ft (1.2m) ↔ 36in (90cm)

Branched stems of slender leaves give this native perennial a bushy, loose habit. Pink buds open to elegant sprays of white star-shaped flowers from summer to autumn.

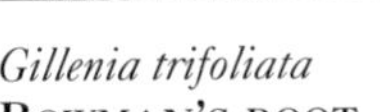

Gillenia trifoliata
Bowman's-root
4-8 ↕ 3ft (1m) ↔ 24in (60cm)

Wiry, reddish stems bear divided, bronze-green leaves and sprays of small white flowers in spring and summer. Decorative red calyces remain after the petals fall.

Kirengeshoma palmata
Kirengeshoma
5-8 ↕ 4ft (1.2m) ↔ 30in (75cm)

A handsome perennial for moist soil with dark stems and large, boldly toothed or lobed leaves. Sprays of waxy, pale yellow flowers open in late summer and autumn.

Kniphofia 'Little Maid'
Torch Lily
5-9 24in (60cm) ↔ 18in (45cm)

Erect stems rise from clumps of grassy leaves in late summer to bear dense spikes of tubular, buff-tinted yellow flowers that are pale green in bud, fading to ivory.

Phlox paniculata 'Fujiyama'
Border Phlox
4-8 ↕ 36in (90cm) ↔ 24in (60cm)

Impressive large heads of snow white flowers crown the stout clumps of upright, leafy stems in late summer. This is one of the best perennials for white flowers.

Phygelius aequalis 'Yellow Trumpet'
Phygelius
7-9 ↕ 3ft (1m) ↔ 4ft (1.2m)

This shrubby perennial has clumps of woody-based, leafy stems bearing loose racemes of drooping, tubular, pale yellow flowers from summer to early autumn.

Trollius x cultorum 'Alabaster'
Globeflower
3-6 ↕ 24in (60cm) ↔ 16in (40cm)

Beautiful, rounded, pale primrose yellow flowers rise on long stems above clumps of long-stalked, lobed, glossy leaves from late spring to summer. It likes moist soil.

Perennials with Fragrant Flowers

IT IS OFTEN SURPRISING to find that a beautiful flower does not have a scent to match. However, most highly fragrant perennials have relatively small flowers and those with large, scented blooms are frequently white or pale colored. Many fragrant flowers are at their best at the end of the day, when night-flying pollinators visit the garden.

Dianthus 'Doris'
PINK
☼ 4-8 ↕↔ 16in (40cm)

Double, pale pink, dark-centered flowers top the bloomy, blue-gray, narrow-leaved stems of this reliable pink during summer and early autumn. It has evergreen leaves.

Hemerocallis 'Marion Vaughn'
DAYLILY
☼ ☀ 4-9 ↕ 34in (85cm) ↔ 30in (75cm)

During summer, clusters of very fragrant, trumpet-shaped, lemon yellow flowers are borne freely on upright stems above bold clumps of narrow, strap-shaped leaves.

Iris graminea
IRIS
☼ ☀ 6-9 ↕ 16in (40cm) ↔ 12in (30cm)

During late spring and early summer, the small, violet-purple flowers of this clump-forming, grassy-leaved iris give off a very distinctive, plumlike fragrance.

PERENNIALS WITH FRAGRANT SPRING FLOWERS

Convallaria majalis
Hyacinthoides non-scripta
Hyacinthus orientalis
Iris reticulata
Iris unguicularis
Muscari spp. and cvs.
Narcissus jonquilla
Narcissus x *odorus*
Petasites fragrans
Phlox divaricata
Viola odorata

Erysimum cheiri 'Blood Red'
ENGLISH WALLFLOWER
☼ 8-9 ↕ 32in (80cm) ↔ 16in (40cm)

These fast-growing, tender perennials are commonly grown as annuals. The sweetly fragrant flowers are available in a number of colors. This one bears rich red blooms.

Hosta 'Honeybells'
HOSTA
☀ ✹ 3-8 ↕ 30in (75cm) ↔ 4ft (1.2m)

This vigorous hosta develops clumps of heart-shaped, veined, and wavy-margined leaves. Fragrant, pale lavender flowers are borne on erect stems in late summer.

Lilium regale
REGAL LILY
☼ 3-8 ↕ 5ft (1.5m) ↔ 16in (40cm)

One of the best known fragrant lilies, this is a must for sunny gardens. Robust stems flaunt clusters of trumpet-shaped white, pink-striped flowers during summer.

Narcissus poeticus var. *recurvus*
POET'S NARCISSUS
☼ ☀ 4-9 ↕ 14in (35cm) ↔ 12in (30cm)

Beautiful, crisp white flowers with pale yellow, red-rimmed cups rise above the narrow, strap-shaped leaves in late spring. In time, it will form clumps.

Nicotiana sylvestris
FLOWERING TOBACCO
☼ ☀ 9-11 ↕ 5ft (1.5m) ↔ 24in (60cm)

The robust, leafy stems carry large heads of long-tubed, fragrant, pure white flowers in summer. A tender perennial generally cultivated as an annual. It will reseed.

PERENNIALS WITH FRAGRANT SUMMER FLOWERS

Dianthus spp. and cvs.
Dictamnus albus, see p.108
Hemerocallis lilioasphodelus
Hesperis matronalis
Hosta plantaginea
Hymenocallis narcissiflora
Lilium candidum
Nepeta x *faassenii*
Paeonia 'Sarah Bernhardt', see p.107
Phlox paniculata

Phlox maculata 'Alpha'
WILD SWEET WILLIAM
☼ ☀ 3-9 ↕ 36in (90cm) ↔ 24in (60cm)

This cultivar of a native phlox produces erect clumps of leafy stems bearing large heads of fragrant pink flowers in summer. It has glossy, mildew-resistant leaves.

Primula auricula var. *albocincta*
AURICULA PRIMROSE
☼ ☀ 2-8 ↕↔ 8in (20cm)

Umbels of fragrant yellow, white-eyed flowers rise above the small clumps of gray-green, white-edged leaves in spring. Excellent for a rock garden or container.

Tulbaghia violacea
SOCIETY GARLIC
☼ 8-11 ↕ 20in (50cm) ↔ 10in (25cm)

Erect stems carry loose umbels of fragrant lilac flowers in summer and early autumn over evergreen clumps of narrow, gray-green leaves. Prefers a warm, sunny site.

Verbena corymbosa 'Gravetye'
VERBENA
☼ 9-11 ↕ 3ft (90cm) ↔ 24in (60cm)

This tender but very attractive perennial produces dense heads of pinkish purple, white-eyed flowers throughout summer that give off a sweet perfume.

Foliage Effect

△ DELICATE CONTRAST *A feathery-leaved* Dicentra *complements the silver-splashed, rounded foliage of a* Lamium.

WHILE MOST FLOWERS bloom for a relatively brief period, foliage can provide a continuous source of drama and atmosphere in the garden. Perennials that have contrasting leaf shapes, textures, and colors will enliven beds and borders. They can also make a striking display as specimen plants.

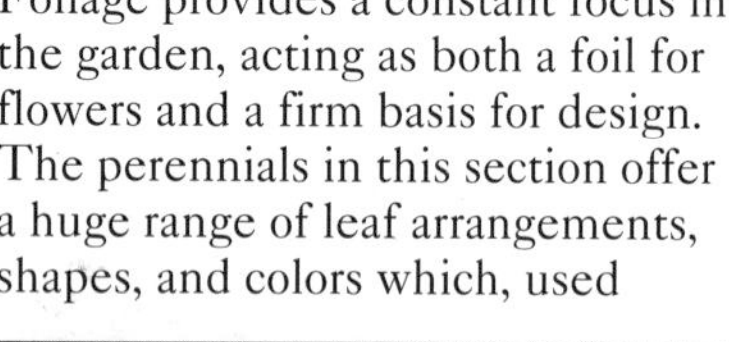

Hosta 'Big Daddy' for bold foliage

Foliage provides a constant focus in the garden, acting as both a foil for flowers and a firm basis for design. The perennials in this section offer a huge range of leaf arrangements, shapes, and colors which, used thoughtfully and with flair, can be combined for spectacular effects. Large-leaved perennials, such as ornamental rhubarbs (*Rheum*), can make impressive specimen plants, or add structure and impact to beds and borders. Foliage perennials will also prove their worth in containers, providing a satisfying, long-lasting display that can be moved around the garden. Richly colored foliage is often associated with autumn, but it is worth remembering that many perennials offer leaves that are attractively variegated or colored for much of the year. Excellent for brightening a dull border, they are also useful for shady sites where other plants may struggle to flower without sufficient sun. In winter, when most other perennials lie below ground, those with evergreen or overwintering leaves, such as heucheras and hardy ferns, can also be used to bring interest and life to the garden landscape.

FOLIAGE CHARACTERISTICS

Leaf arrangements, shapes, and colors are all important elements to consider when combining foliage perennials for eye-catching contrasts and effects.

ARRANGEMENT *of leaves is a characteristic feature of every plant. Exploit this to bring structure and texture to the garden.*

SHAPE AND SIZE *can be contrasted for extra interest. Leaves with jagged, feathery, or spiny margins will all create different effects.*

COLOR *in foliage can be used to create a calm, dark backdrop, or to bring brightness and warmth to shady sites in the garden.*

◁ COLOR CONTAINER *Yellow-striped* Hakonechloa *and blue-leaved* Acaena *contrast here with upright* Imperata.

▷ DRAMATIC LEAVES *Perennials with bold foliage make good specimen plants or can be used to great effect in a border.*

Perennials with Evergreen or Overwintering Foliage

In winter, when most herbaceous perennials have died down to below ground level and no longer provide a focus in the garden, it is important to have at least a scattering of plants with evergreen leaves or foliage that overwinters in an attractive state. Even when flowerless, these plants will bring continual color and interest to any garden.

Asarum europaeum
EUROPEAN WILD GINGER
☼ ☀ 4-8 ↕3in (8cm) ↔12in (30cm)

One of the best perennial groundcovers, and attractive all year round. During late spring, the dense carpet of kidney-shaped, glossy leaves hides curious little flowers.

Helleborus argutifolius
CORSICAN HELLEBORE
☼ ☼ 7-8 ↕↔36in (90cm)

This handsome plant can be admired all year. Pale green, overwintering stems bear beautifully veined, prickle-toothed leaves and apple green flowers in late winter.

Kniphofia caulescens
RED HOT POKER
☼ ☼ 6-9 ↕4ft (1.2m) ↔36in (90cm)

An impressive perennial producing large clumps of fine-toothed, blue-green leaves topped in late summer by imposing coral red flower spikes that fade to yellow.

Bergenia cordifolia 'Purpurea'
BERGENIA
☼ ☼ 3-9 ↕24in (60cm) ↔30in (75cm)

The leathery, rounded, deep green leaves form a low patch and turn purple- or red-tinted in winter. Stems of magenta-purple flowers emerge during early spring.

Iris foetidissima 'Variegata'
STINKING IRIS
☼ ☼ 6-9 ↕↔24in (60cm)

A superb, variegated form of the species with evergreen, strap-shaped, shiny leaves boldly margined in white. Orange seedheads follow the purple summer flowers.

Phormium cookianum subsp. *hookeri* 'Tricolor'
☼ 9-11 ↕↔6ft (2m)

A colorful tender perennial eventually forming a large mound of arching, glossy green leaves with creamy yellow and red margins. It can be overwintered indoors.

Polypodium vulgare 'Cornubiense'
COMMON POLYPODY
☼ ☀ 5-8 ↕↔ 16in (40cm)

The deeply divided, rich green fronds of this vigorous, creeping fern make it an excellent groundcover. It is also suitable for a rock garden, wall, or container.

Pulmonaria saccharata 'Leopard'
PULMONARIA
☀ ☀ 3-8 ↕ 12in (30cm) ↔ 24in (60cm)

Silvery-spotted, semievergreen foliage makes this perennial particularly effective groundcover. Violet-red flowers are borne during late winter and early spring.

Tellima grandiflora
FRINGE CUPS
☀ 4-8 ↕ 32in (80cm) ↔ 12in (30cm)

Semievergreen clumps of long-stalked, heart-shaped, hairy and scalloped leaves are topped by handsome, loose spikes of greenish white flowers during spring.

OTHER EVERGREEN OR OVERWINTERING PERENNIALS

Arum italicum
Carex morrowii 'Variegata'
Chiastophyllum oppositifolium
Dryopteris intermedia
Equisetum hyemale
Galax urceolata
Helichtotrichon sempervirens, see p.131
Helleborus orientalis
Iberis sempervirens
Lavandula angustifolia
Liriope muscari 'Variegata'
Phlomis russeliana
Polypodium spp. and cvs.
Polystichum munitum, see p.140
Polystichum acrostichoides
Santolina chamaecyparissus
Sasa veitchii, see p.135
Yucca filamentosa

Vinca minor 'Argenteovariegata'
COMMON PERIWINKLE
☼ ☀ 4-9 ↕ 6in (15cm) ↔ indefinite

All periwinkles are useful groundcovers, but this also has leaves with attractive, creamy white margins. Pale violet-blue flowers emerge in spring and autumn.

Perennials with Strap- or Sword-shaped Leaves

PERENNIALS THAT FORM CLUMPS of long, slender leaves are irresistible and always striking. Regardless of whether the leaves stand stiff and upright, or bend and arch in a more graceful manner, they are invaluable for contrasting with more conventional, broad-leaved perennials in beds or borders. They can also be used as dramatic specimen plants.

Iris pseudacorus 'Variegata'
YELLOW FLAG
☼ ☀ 4-9 ↕↔ 4ft (1.2m)

A vigorous iris for wet sites forming a large patch of tall green leaves with bold white or creamy yellow bands. Yellow flowers are borne on erect stems during summer.

Arundo donax 'Macrophylla'
GIANT REED
☼ 5-9 ↕ 15ft (5m) ↔ 6ft (2m)

This giant grass produces long, arching, slender, glaucous leaves and bamboolike stems that flaunt feathery plumes in summer. It prefers a warm, sheltered site.

Eryngium agavifolium
ERYNGIUM
☼ 7-9 ↕ 4ft (1.2m) ↔ 24in (60cm)

The sharply toothed, glossy, evergreen leaves form a striking, erect clump above which sturdy stems carry cylindrical heads of tiny, greenish white flowers in summer.

EVERGREEN AND SEMIEVERGREEN PERENNIALS WITH STRAP- OR SWORD-SHAPED LEAVES

Acorus gramineus
Crocosmia paniculata
Eryngium eburneum, see p.22
Eryngium pandanifolium
Hemerocallis aurantiaca
Iris foetidissima 'Variegata', see p.114
Watsonia pillansii
Yucca filamentosa
Yucca recurvifolia

Crocosmia 'Lucifer'
CROCOSMIA
☼ ☀ 5-9 ↕ 4ft (1.2m) ↔ 18in (45cm)

A bright and cheerful perennial forming a clump of robust, sword-shaped leaves. Its arching, branched spikes of brilliant red, late-summer flowers are good for cutting.

Hemerocallis 'Gentle Shepherd'
DAYLILY
☼ ☀ 4-9 ↕ 26in (65cm) ↔ 4ft (1.2m)

Bold clumps of semievergreen, narrow, arching green leaves are topped by ivory-white, trumpet-shaped flowers with green throats during summer.

Iris sibirica 'Perry's Blue'
IRIS
☼ ☀ 2-9 ↕ 4ft (1.2m) ↔ 3ft (1m)

Erect clumps of narrow, grasslike leaves are topped by blue-violet flowers on erect, soldierlike stems in early summer. The winter seed capsules are also decorative.

Kniphofia 'Wrexham Buttercup'
TORCH LILY
☼ 5-9 ↕ 4ft (1.2m) ↔ 24in (60cm)

The long, arching, narrow green leaves of this perennial form a dense clump. Its pokerlike heads of rich yellow flowers are carried on strong, erect stems in summer.

Persicaria macrophylla
PERSICARIA
☼ ◑ 5-8 ↕↔ 12in (30cm)

A semievergreen perennial with lance-shaped, conspicuously veined leaves and dense spikes of pink to red flowers borne through summer into autumn.

Phormium tenax
NEW ZEALAND FLAX
☼ 9-11 ↕ 12ft (4m) ↔ 6ft (2m)

Few perennials are as eye-catching as this one with its sword-shaped, glaucous gray, evergreen leaves and statuesque panicles of waxy, dark red flowers in summer.

Sisyrinchium striatum 'Aunt May'
SISYRINCHIUM
☼ 7-8 ↕ 20in (50cm) ↔ 12in (30cm)

This irislike perennial has striking fans of sword-shaped, gray-green leaves boldly striped creamy yellow. In summer, it bears straw yellow flowers in stiff spikes.

Yucca flaccida
YUCCA
☼ 6-9 ↕ 22in (55cm) ↔ 5ft (1.5m)

Reliable and evergreen, this yucca forms a bold rosette of narrow, dark blue-green leaves with wispy marginal fibers. Large spikes of ivory flowers emerge in summer.

HERBACEOUS PERENNIALS WITH STRAP- OR SWORD-SHAPED LEAVES

Belamcanda chinensis
Carex siderosticha 'Variegata', see p.138
Elymus arenarius
Eremurus stenophyllus, see p.33
Eryngium yuccifolium
Gladiolus communis subsp. *byzantinus*, see p. 33
Hemerocallis fulva
Iris Bearded Hybrids
Liatris spicata
Pyrrosia lingua
Tradescantia virginiana

Perennials with Jagged or Deeply Cut Leaves

A SUBTLE, YET EFFECTIVE WAY to add contrast and texture to a planting is to combine plants with different leaf shapes. Plants with deeply cut or jaggedly cut foliage are especially effective contrasted with bold, entire leaves. Many of these plants have the added advantage of attractive flowers.

Astilbe simplicifolia 'Bronze Elegans'
ASTILBE
☼ ☀ 5-8 ↕ 12in (30cm) ↔ 10in (25cm)

One of the smallest and daintiest astilbes forming mounds of ferny, glossy, dark green leaves. In summer, it produces neat little plumes of pinkish red flowers.

Incarvillea delavayi
HARDY GLOXINIA
☼ ☀ 6-8 ↕ 24in (60cm) ↔ 12in (30cm)

Attractive clumps of bold, deeply divided, dark green leaves are truly eye-catching in summer when topped with erect stems of trumpet-shaped, rose-pink flowers.

Cimicifuga simplex Atropurpurea Group
KAMCHATKA BUGBANE
☀ 3-8 ↕ 4ft (1.2m) ↔ 24in (60cm)

The loose clumps of large, much-divided, dark green to purplish leaves are topped in autumn by cylindrical, dark-stemmed racemes of tiny white flowers.

Ligularia przewalskii
LIGULARIA
☼ ☀ 3-8 ↕ 6ft (2m) ↔ 3ft (1m)

This perennial has large clumps of sharply divided, deeply cut, rounded leaves. The dark-stemmed spires of yellow flowers are borne in summer. Requires moist soil.

Rodgersia henrici
RODGERSIA
☼ ☀ 5-8 ↕↔ 3ft (1m)

All rodgersias sport handsome foliage, but this one is particularly desirable. It has large, horsechestnut-like leaves and pink or white flower plumes in summer.

Senecio tanguticus
CHINESE RAGWORT
☼ ☀ 4-7 ↕ 4ft (1.2m) ↔ indefinite

Creeping rootstocks produce stout, dark stems clothed in jaggedly cut leaves. In autumn, conical heads of yellow flowers emerge. This plant can be invasive.

OTHER PERENNIALS WITH JAGGED OR DEEPLY CUT LEAVES

- *Acanthus spinosus*, see p.120
- *Aconitum* spp. and cvs.
- *Astrantia major*
- *Eryngium amethystinum*
- *Kirengeshoma palmata*, see p.109
- *Podophyllum peltatum*
- *Rheum palmatum* var. *tanguticum*, see p.123
- *Rodgersia pinnata*, see p.61
- *Rodgersia podophylla*, see p.133

Perennials with Feathery Foliage

MANY FERNS AND SOME PERENNIALS have leaves so finely divided that they create a striking feathery effect in the garden – the perfect foil for more dramatic foliage or for hot-colored flowers, which stand out against the delicate leaves. Many will also make excellent specimen plants in containers or in a prominent garden site.

Adiantum pedatum
MAIDENHAIR FERN
2-8 ↕↔ 16in (40cm)

Given time and a sheltered, moist site, this lovely, hardy native fern will develop a large clump of slender, glossy black stalks with delicate, much-divided fronds.

Corydalis cheilanthifolia
CORYDALIS
5-7 ↕ 12in (30cm) ↔ 10in (25cm)

Each finely divided, orange-tinted leaf is like a green feather. Slender racemes of deep yellow flowers are borne in spring and summer. It will seed around if happy.

Meum athamanticum
BALDMONEY, SPIGNEL
5-8 ↕ 18in (45cm) ↔ 12in (30cm)

Like fennel, this plant is a member of the carrot family, with similar feathery, deeply divided, aromatic leaves. Dense heads of tiny white flowers are borne in summer.

OTHER PERENNIALS WITH FEATHERY FOLIAGE

Achillea millefolium
Artemisia ludoviciana
Astilbe spp. and cvs.
Athyrium filix-femina, see p.140
Dicentra eximia
Myrrhis odorata, see p.49
Paesia scaberula
Paeonia tenuifolia, see p.149
Polystichum setiferum, see p.140
Pulsatilla vulgaris

Aruncus aethusifolius
ARUNCUS
4-7 ↕ 10in (25cm) ↔ 16in (40cm)

A charming plant producing small mounds of finely divided, crisp green leaves that turn orange or yellow in autumn. Small white flower plumes are borne in summer.

Foeniculum vulgare 'Purpureum'
PURPLE FENNEL
5-9 ↕ 6ft (1.8m) ↔ 18in (45cm)

This aromatic fennel has attractive, finely divided, plumed leaves that are bronze-purple when young, aging to blue-green. Flat yellow flowerheads open in summer.

Onychium japonicum
CARROT FERN
9-11 ↕ 20in (50cm) ↔ 12in (30cm)

An elegant tender fern producing a dense clump of finely divided, bright green fronds on slender, wiry stalks. In northern zones, this fern is grown under glass.

Perennials with Spiny Leaves

THE JAGGED EFFECT of spiny or prickly-leaved plants has a definite appeal for some gardeners. Often architectural in habit as well as ornamental, these distinctive perennials can bring structure to borders or make bold specimens. Many are particularly useful for dry sites, as their spiny leaves are specially adapted to minimize water loss.

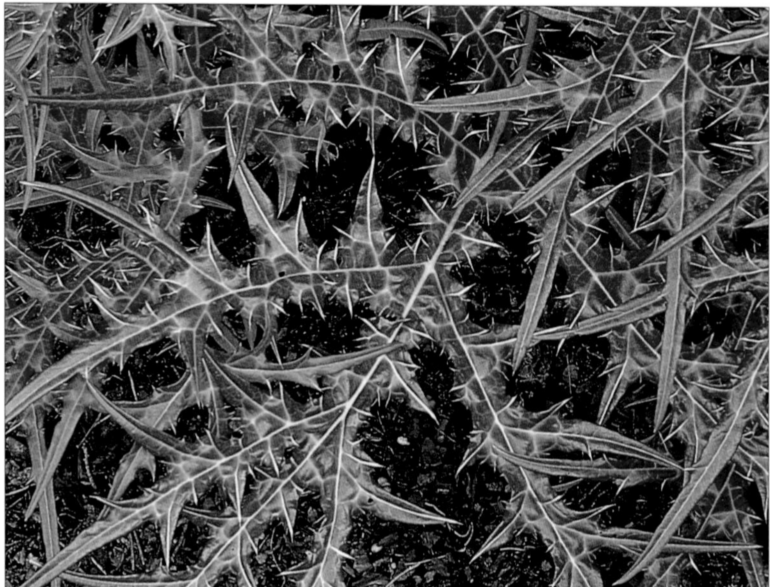

Acanthus spinosus
SPINY BEAR'S-BREECH
☼ ☀ 7-10 ↕ 4ft (1.2m) ↔ 24in (60cm)

The large, deeply divided, green or gray-green leaves have white midribs and spiny margins. Tall racemes of purple-bracted white flowers open in spring and summer.

Aciphylla aurea
GOLDEN SPANIARD
☼ 8-10 ↕↔ 3ft (1m)

This slow-growing, evergreen plant forms an imposing rosette of stiff, spine-tipped, deeply divided, gray-green leaves with bold, golden yellow midribs and margins.

Eryngium maritimum
SEA HOLLY
☼ 5-8 ↕↔ 12in (30cm)

Found in maritime sands or gravels in the wild, this sea holly has formidably spiny, deeply lobed, leathery, bloomy, blue-gray leaves. Pale blue flowers open in summer.

Eryngium variifolium
SEA HOLLY
☼ 5-9 ↕ 14in (35cm) ↔ 10in (25cm)

A beautiful evergreen forming a rosette of rounded, silver-veined leaves. In summer, erect, branched stems bear small, gray-blue flowerheads with spiny white collars.

OTHER PERENNIALS WITH SPINY LEAVES

Agave havardiana
Berkheya macrocephala
Cynara cardunculus, see p.130
Dasylirion wheeleri
Echinops sphaerocephalus
Eryngium bourgatii, see p.20
Eryngium eburneum, see p.22
Sabal minor
Yucca gloriosa, see p.31
Yucca rupicola

Puya chilensis
PUYA
☼ 10-11 ↕ 12ft (4m) ↔ 6ft (2m)

After several years, a tall, stout stem with a head of waxy, yellow-green flowers rises from the massive rosette of rapierlike, spine-toothed, leathery, evergreen leaves.

Perennials with Aromatic Leaves

SCENTS CAN MAKE an important and evocative contribution to a garden and are most commonly associated with the fragrance of flowers. The leaves of most perennials, however, also give off at least a faint aroma, and some even have foliage with a very distinctive or strong scent. In some cases, this is released by simply brushing against the plant.

Agastache foeniculum 'Alabaster'
ANISE HYSSOP
☼ 6-9 ↕36in (90cm) ↔12in (30cm)

Downy, anise-scented leaves, paler green beneath, clothe the erect stems. Spikes of two-lipped white flowers, loved by bees, are borne from midsummer to autumn.

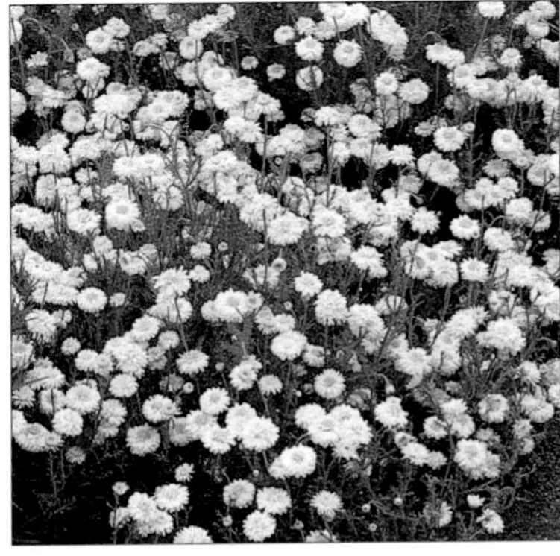

Chamaemelum nobile 'Flore Pleno'
DOUBLE CHAMOMILE
☼ 4-8 ↕12in (30cm) ↔18in (45cm)

This small, creeping, aromatic perennial produces dense mats of finely divided, hairy leaves. Long-stalked, double white flowers are borne freely in summer.

Helichrysum italicum
CURRY PLANT
☼ 8-9 ↕24in (60cm) ↔36in (90cm)

Aromatic, evergreen, narrow, felted, silver-gray leaves clothe the woolly stems of this woody-based perennial or subshrub. Deep yellow flower clusters open in summer.

Melissa officinalis
LEMON BALM
☼ ◑ 4-9 ↕3ft (1m) ↔24in (60cm)

When rubbed, the leaves of this bushy perennial release a sharp lemon aroma. In summer, its four-angled stems bear spikes of pale yellow flowers that fade to white.

Nepeta 'Six Hills Giant'
CATMINT
☼ ◑ 3-8 ↕36in (90cm) ↔24in (60cm)

This dense, bushy, clump-forming plant bears aromatic, light gray-green leaves and leafy spikes of lavender-blue summer flowers. Loved, but also damaged, by cats.

OTHER PERENNIALS WITH AROMATIC LEAVES

Acorus calamus 'Variegatus'
Artemisia absinthium
Dictamnus albus, see p.108
Foeniculum vulgare 'Purpureum', see p.119
Lavandula angustifolia
Mentha spp. and cvs.
Monarda didyma
Myrrhis odorata, see p.49
Origanum vulgare
Perovskia atriplicifolia
Thymus spp. and cvs.

Salvia officinalis 'Icterina'
GARDEN SAGE
☼ 3-9 ↕↔12in (30cm)

An ornamental variegated form of the popular kitchen-garden herb forming a low, woody-based mound of attractive, aromatic, woolly, green-and-yellow leaves.

Perennials with Bold Leaves

PERENNIALS WITH BOLD LEAVES, whether broad like those of hostas or deeply cut and fernlike, provide gardens with some of the most memorable show-stoppers. In sites where space is no object, they are eye-catching planted in groups or drifts. They can be just as successful, and possibly even more dramatic, as single specimens in smaller gardens.

OTHER HERBACEOUS PERENNIALS WITH BOLD LEAVES

Acanthus mollis
Agave havardiana
Darmera peltata, see p.60
Filipendula kamtschatica
Gunnera manicata
Hosta sieboldiana and cvs.
Inula magnifica
Polygonatum commutatum
Polygonatum odoratum 'Variegatum'
Rodgersia aesculifolia, see p.19

Aralia cachemirica
ARALIA
☼ ☀ 6-9 ↕10ft (3m) ↔6ft (2m)

Given a good site, this aralia forms a huge, suckering clump of large, arching, divided leaves. Black berries follow tall, branched heads of tiny flowers in early summer.

Dicksonia antarctica
AUSTRALIAN TREE FERN
☀ ● 9-11 ↕20ft (6m) ↔12ft (4m)

This majestic, evergreen fern has a single rhizome forming a false, erect trunk that is clothed in a dense, thick mass of roots and crowned on top with a huge ruff of fronds.

Astilboides tabularis
ASTILBOIDES
☀ 5-7 ↕5ft (1.5m) ↔4ft (1.2m)

In summer, slender plumes of tiny, creamy white flowers rise above the large clumps of huge, rounded, sharply lobed leaves. It enjoys a site with moist to boggy soil.

OTHER TENDER PERENNIALS WITH BOLD LEAVES

Arum creticum, see p.32
Beschorneria yuccoides
Brugmansia spp. and cvs.
Canna 'Assault', see p.64
Geranium maderense
Pelargonium spp. and cvs.
Phormium cookianum subsp. *hookeri* 'Tricolor', see p.114
Phormium tenax, see p.117
Wachendorfia thyrsiflora

Filipendula purpurea
MEADOWSWEET
☼ ☀ 4-9 ↕4ft (1.2m) ↔24in (60cm)

Large, deeply lobed and toothed leaves cover the bold clumps of upright, crimson-purple stems. Tall, branched plumes of carmine-red flowers are borne in summer.

Geranium palmatum
CRANESBILL
☼ ☀ 8-10 ↕↔ 3ft (1m)

Branched heads of purplish pink flowers top the large rosettes of semievergreen, long-stalked, deeply lobed, sharp-toothed leaves in summer.

Hosta 'Big Daddy'
HOSTA
☀ ● 3-9 ↕ 24in (60cm) ↔ 3ft (1m)

Aptly named, this hosta forms mounded clumps of large, rounded to heart-shaped, veined and puckered, blue-gray leaves. White flowers are borne during summer.

Rheum 'Ace of Hearts'
ORNAMENTAL RHUBARB
☼ ☀ 5-9 ↕ 4ft (1.2m) ↔ 36in (90cm)

The impressive mounds of heart-shaped leaves are red-veined above and purple-red beneath. Branching stems carry sprays of pale pinkish white flowers in summer.

Rheum palmatum var. *tanguticum*
ORNAMENTAL RHUBARB
☼ ☀ 5-9 ↕ 8ft (2.5m) ↔ 6ft (1.8m)

The striking, huge, toothed and jaggedly lobed leaves are red-suffused when young. In summer, branched heads of white, red, or pink flowers emerge. Superb by water.

Symplocarpus foetidus
SKUNK CABBAGE
☼ ☀ 3-7 ↕↔ 24in (60cm)

Curious, hooded, purplish red flowers in spring are followed by the clump of large, rather leathery leaves. An excellent bog plant, it needs plenty of moisture.

Telekia speciosa
TELEKIA
☀ 5-8 ↕ 6ft (2m) ↔ 4ft (1.2m)

This strapping plant forms a large patch of branching stems that bear heart-shaped leaves. Rich yellow, brown-centered, daisy heads appear in late summer and autumn.

Veratrum viride
INDIAN POKE
☼ ☀ 3-7 ↕ 6ft (2m) ↔ 24in (60cm)

The clumps of pleated, rich green leaves that emerge in spring are more striking than the tall, branched spikes of yellowish green, star-shaped summer flowers.

Perennials with Yellow- or Gold-variegated Foliage

VARIEGATED PERENNIALS AND ORNAMENTAL GRASSES that have leaves blotched or spotted with yellow or gold are prized for their ability to bring warmth and light to plantings dominated by dark green foliage. Many also make impressive specimen plants on their own, grown either in containers or in small beds.

Aquilegia vulgaris Vervaeneana Group
EUROPEAN COLUMBINE
☼ ☀ 3-9 ↕36in (90cm) ↔18in (45cm)

The rounded, divided leaves are streaked and mottled yellow in this curious form of an old cottage-garden favorite. Spring or summer flowers are white, pink, or purple.

Carex hachijoensis 'Evergold'
EVERGOLD JAPANESE SEDGE
☼ ☀ 7-9 ↕12in (30cm) ↔14in (35cm)

This bright little evergreen sedge forms a dense, low clump of handsome, arching, grasslike foliage. Each dark green leaf has a broad, creamy yellow central stripe.

Convallaria majalis 'Hardwick Hall'
LILY-OF-THE-VALLEY
☼ 4-9 ↕9in (23cm) ↔12in (30cm)

A choice form of a much-loved perennial that slowly forms patches of attractively veined, bright green leaves with narrow, paler margins. It has white spring flowers.

Cortaderia selloana 'Aureolineata'
PAMPAS GRASS
☼ 8-11 ↕7ft (2.2m) ↔5ft (1.5m)

A variegated form of a familiar, evergreen grass producing huge mounds of arching, saw-toothed, yellow-margined leaves. Tall flower plumes in summer are a bonus.

Hakonechloa macra 'Aureola'
HAKONE GRASS
☼ ☀ 5-9 ↕14in (35cm) ↔16in (40cm)

One of the most pleasing of all grasses, with low mounds of yellow, green-striped leaves. In autumn, it bears airy panicles of spikelets and the leaves flush red.

OTHER YELLOW- OR GOLD-VARIEGATED PERENNIALS

Gaura lindheimeri 'Corrie's Gold'
Hosta 'Golden Tiara', see p.145
Hosta 'Kabitan'
Hosta montana 'Aureomarginata', see p.145
Hosta ventricosa 'Aureomaculata'
Liriope muscari 'Variegata'
Mentha x *gracilis* 'Variegata'
Salvia officinalis 'Aurea'
Yucca smalliana 'Bright Edge'

Hosta 'Gold Standard'
HOSTA
☀ 3-8 ↕26in (65cm) ↔3ft (1m)

This singularly attractive perennial forms clumps of heart-shaped, greenish yellow leaves fading to green margins. Tall stems bear lavender-blue flowers in summer.

Hosta ventricosa 'Variegata'
HOSTA
3-9 ↕20in (50cm) ↔3ft (1m)

Big, bold clumps of heart-shaped, deep-veined green leaves have irregular yellow margins aging to creamy white. Tall stems carry deep purple flowers in summer.

Iris pallida 'Variegata'
SWEET IRIS
4-8 ↕4ft (1.2m) ↔24in (60cm)

An effective variegated perennial with stout clumps of sword-shaped, gray-green or green leaves striped light yellow. In late spring, it bears scented, soft blue flowers.

Miscanthus sinensis 'Zebrinus'
ZEBRA GRASS
5-9 ↕↔4ft (1.2m)

This ornamental grass is very popular for specimen planting. The bold clumps of slender, canelike stems bear long, narrow green leaves banded white or pale yellow.

Symphytum 'Goldsmith'
COMFREY
4-9 ↕↔12in (30cm)

A superb groundcover, this creeping plant forms large patches of hairy leaves with irregular gold or cream margins. Blue and white, pink-tinted flowers occur in spring.

Tolmiea menziesii 'Taff's Gold'
PIGGY-BACK PLANT
6-9 ↕20in (50cm) ↔24in (60cm)

Loose clumps of semievergreen, hairy, maplelike leaves are pale green, spotted and blotched cream and pale yellow. The tiny flowers are of little consequence.

Trifolium pratense 'Susan Smith'
CLOVER
7-10 ↕6in (15cm) ↔18in (45cm)

The characteristic clover leaves of this mat-forming perennial have green leaflets that are curiously but attractively netted with golden yellow veins.

Yucca flaccida 'Golden Sword'
YUCCA
4-11 ↕5ft (1.5m) ↔3ft (1m)

A bold, clump-forming evergreen bearing stiff, swordlike, blue-green leaves with central yellow bands. Panicles of white bell-shaped flowers open in late summer.

OTHER YELLOW-STRIPED GRASSES

Arundo donax 'Variegata'
Carex morrowii 'Gold Band'
x *Hibanobambusa tranquilans* 'Shirobana'
Miscanthus sinensis 'Goldfeder'
Miscanthus sinensis 'Univittatus'
Molinia caerulea 'Variegata'
Phalaris arundinacea var. *picta* 'Luteopicta'
Pleioblastus auricomus

Perennials with White- or Cream-variegated Foliage

IT IS A CURIOUS FACT that there are far more perennials with white- or cream-variegated foliage than with yellow or gold variegation. Patterned with stripes, spots, blotches, marbling, or marginal lines, these leaves provide a useful contrast for plants with green or purple foliage, and can brighten up dark corners or dull combinations in the garden.

Armoracia rusticana 'Variegata'
HORSERADISH
☼ 5-9 ↕ 3ft (1m) ↔ 18in (45cm)

This variegated form of the well-known herb has clumps of large, coarse, wholly or partially white leaves. Branched stems of white flowers appear during summer.

Convallaria majalis 'Albostriata'
LILY-OF-THE-VALLEY
☀ 4-9 ↕ 9in (23cm) ↔ 12in (30cm)

The leaves of this favorite garden plant are striped lengthwise with creamy white. Sprays of nodding, fragrant, bell-shaped white flowers are borne in spring.

Hemerocallis fulva 'Kwanzo Variegata'
DAYLILY
☼ 2-9 ↕ 30in (75cm) ↔ 4ft (1.2m)

Long, strap-shaped, arching leaves with white stripes form a bold clump. Double, tawny orange flowers rise above the foliage on strong, erect stems in summer.

Brunnera macrophylla 'Dawson's White'
SIBERIAN BUGLOSS
☀ 3-8 ↕ 18in (45cm) ↔ 24in (60cm)

Low mounds of softly-hairy, heart-shaped leaves are irregularly margined in creamy white. Sprays of bright blue, forget-me-not flowers rise over the foliage in spring.

Euphorbia characias subsp. *wulfenii* 'Burrow Silver'
☼ 7-9 ↕↔ 4ft (1.2m)

Bushy and woody-based, this evergreen has dense, gray-green leaves with creamy margins. Rounded heads of bright yellow-green flowers open in spring and summer.

Hosta 'Shade Fanfare'
HOSTA
☀ 3-9 ↕ 18in (45cm) ↔ 24in (60cm)

An excellent groundcover that produces clumps of bold, heart-shaped leaves with irregular cream-white margins. Lavender-blue flowers are borne in summer.

Phlox paniculata 'Harlequin'
Garden Phlox
☼ 4-8 ↕4ft (1.2m) ↔3ft (1m)

Robust clumps of erect stems bear leaves boldly margined in creamy white. Showy panicles of fragrant, red-purple flowers open in summer.

Symphytum x *uplandicum* 'Variegatum'
Comfrey
☼ ☼ 4-9 ↕36in (90cm) ↔24in (60cm)

A tough, deep-rooted perennial producing a spectacular clump of white-margined leaves. In summer, striking variegated stems bear blue and pink flowers.

Other Perennials with White- or Cream-variegated Foliage

Ajuga reptans 'Silver Beauty'
Hosta 'White Christmas'
Iris pallida 'Argentea Variegata', see p.67
Mentha suaveolens 'Variegata'
Miscanthus sinensis 'Cabaret', see p.139
Polygonatum odoratum 'Variegatum'
Sedum erythrostictum 'Mediovariegatum'

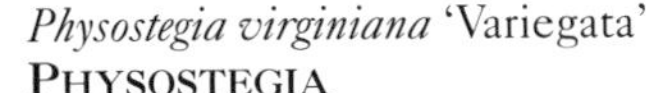

Physostegia virginiana 'Variegata'
Physostegia
☼ ☼ 3-9 ↕↔18in (45cm)

The willowlike leaves of this easily grown perennial, borne on erect stems, are gray-green, variegated white. Magenta-pink flower spikes emerge in late summer.

Myosotis scorpioides 'Maytime'
Forget-me-not
☼ 3-8 ↕↔12in (30cm)

Strikingly variegated, this waterside plant forms patches of white-margined leaves. Sprays of bright blue flowers open in early summer. Needs a constantly moist site.

Pulmonaria 'Roy Davidson'
Lungwort
☼ ☼ 3-9 ↕12in (30cm) ↔24in (60cm)

A good groundcover with clumps of semi-evergreen, roughly-hairy, white-spotted leaves. Clusters of tubular, blue and pink flowers appear in spring. It will self-seed.

Vinca major 'Variegata'
Large Periwinkle
☼ ☼ 7-9 ↕18in (45cm) ↔6ft (2m)

This fast-growing, scrambling evergreen forms blankets of striking, paired, creamy white-margined leaves. Pale blue flowers appear from late spring through summer.

Perennials with Yellow or Gold Foliage

A SURPRISING NUMBER of garden perennials have produced sports with yellow or gold leaves. In some plants, the best foliage effect is achieved in spring; in others, the color is retained throughout summer. All have an important role in the garden, especially in shady or dimly lit corners, or as a contrast to greens and purples.

Aquilegia 'Mellow Yellow'
COLUMBINE
3-9 ↕24in (60cm) ↔18in (45cm)

An attractive form of a popular perennial with golden leaves in spring that pale to yellow-green in summer, when pretty, white to pale blue flowers are produced.

Carex elata 'Aurea'
BOWLES' GOLDEN SEDGE
5-9 ↕28in (70cm) ↔36in (90cm)

This clump-forming sedge has arching, grassy, bright golden leaves. Probably the best golden-leaved perennial for waterside sites, it is superb by streams or pools.

Hosta 'Midas Touch'
PLANTAIN LILY
3-9 ↕20in (50cm) ↔26in (65cm)

There are many golden-leaved hostas available, but this is one of the best. It has big, bold, handsomely corrugated foliage and bears lavender-blue summer flowers.

Lamium maculatum 'Cannon's Gold'
GOLDEN SPOTTED LAMIUM
3-8 ↕8in (20cm) ↔3ft (1m)

The coarsely toothed, semievergreen leaves of this lamium form a soft yellow carpet in spring and summer. Its mauve-pink flowers emerge in early summer.

Campanula garganica 'Dickson's Gold'
GARANGO BELLFLOWER
6-8 ↕2in (5cm) ↔12in (30cm)

This cheerful perennial forms a mound of neat little toothed, kidney-shaped leaves. These turn golden in summer at the same time as small blue flowers appear.

Centaurea montana 'Gold Bullion'
PERENNIAL CORNFLOWER
3-8 ↕18in (45cm) ↔24in (60cm)

A beautiful, golden-leaved version of an old garden favorite. The pronounced leaf color during spring and early summer is a perfect foil for the large blue flowers.

Lysimachia nummularia 'Aurea'
GOLDEN CREEPING JENNY
3-8 ↕2in (5cm) ↔indefinite

One of the brightest and most reliable golden-leaved plants, its round leaves on creeping stems turn greenish yellow in shade. Yellow flowers emerge in summer.

Melissa officinalis 'All Gold'
LEMON BALM
☼ 4-9 ↕↔ 24in (60cm)

This bushy, aromatic perennial produces a dense clump of lemon-scented, yellow-green stems and leaves. It is especially effective during spring and early summer.

Stachys byzantina 'Primrose Heron'
LAMB'S-EARS
☼ 4-8 ↕ 18in (45cm) ↔ 24in (60cm)

A vigorous, semievergreen plant forming a dense carpet of velvety, hairy gray stems and woolly leaves that are yellow-green during spring and early summer.

Tanacetum vulgare 'Isla Gold'
GOLDEN TANSY
☼ 3-8 ↕↔ 36in (90cm)

This golden form of the common tansy has bold clumps of erect stems clothed in aromatic, finely divided, yellowy leaves. It bears yellow flowerheads in summer.

Tradescantia x *andersoniana* 'Blue and Gold'
☼ ☀ 3-9 ↕↔ 18in (45cm)

During summer, rich blue, three-petaled flowers on erect, fleshy stems contrast well with this clump-forming perennial's long, strap-shaped, yellow-green leaves.

Valeriana phu 'Aurea'
GOLDEN VALERIAN
☼ ☀ 5-8 ↕ 5ft (1.5m) ↔ 24in (60cm)

The prime attraction of this tall, branching perennial is its gold spring foliage, which gradually fades to green in summer. Its small white flowers open in late summer.

OTHER PERENNIALS WITH GOLD FOLIAGE

Acanthus mollis 'Hollard's Gold'
Acorus gramineus 'Ogon'
Carex elata 'Bowles' Golden'
Filipendula ulmaria 'Aurea'
Hosta 'Golden Sculpture'
Hosta 'Sum and Substance', see p.65
Hosta 'Zounds', see p.60
Lamium maculatum 'Golden Nuggets'
Luzula sylvatica 'Aurea'
Origanum vulgare 'Aureum', see p.49
Melissa officinalis 'Aurea', see p.49
Milium effusum 'Aureum', see p.27
Saxifraga exarata subsp. *moschata* 'Cloth of Gold'
Symphytum ibericum 'Gold in Spring'
Thymus x *citriodorus* 'Archer's Gold'
Tricyrtis 'Lemon Lime'
Veronica prostrata 'Trehane'

Perennials with Silver or Blue-gray Foliage

PERENNIALS THAT HAVE SILVER or blue-gray foliage are invaluable in the garden for separating strong-colored plants, such as those with red, purple, or even plain green leaves. They can also provide a lovely foil for pastel-colored flowers, especially those in pink, lavender-purple, pale blue, and yellow. There is a vast number of perennials to choose from for a gray or silver bed or border. They can also make a spectacular display as specimen plants or grouped together with other contrasting foliage plants in containers. Most perennials with silver leaves prefer to be grown in a warm, sunny situation.

Anaphalis triplinervis 'Sommerschnee'
PEARLY EVERLASTING
☼ 3-8 ↕ 32in (80cm) ↔ 24in (60cm)

The clumps of gray stems bear leaves that are woolly white beneath. In late summer, dense white flower clusters emerge. A German selection of a reliable perennial.

Artemisia ludoviciana var. *albula*
ARTEMISIA
☼ 3-9 ↕ 4ft (1.2m) ↔ 24in (60cm)

Erect clumps of slender, woolly stems bear willowlike, aromatic, woolly white leaves. Dense clusters of white flowers are borne from summer into autumn.

Cerastium tomentosum
SNOW-IN-SUMMER
☼ 2-7 ↕ 3in (8cm) ↔ 5ft (1.5m)

One of the best gray groundcover plants for walls and sunny banks. During late spring and summer, white flowers pepper the carpet of evergreen, downy leaves.

Crambe maritima
SEA KALE
☼ 6-9 ↕ 30in (75cm) ↔ 24in (60cm)

This bold, mound-forming plant has large, deeply lobed and twisted, bloomy, blue-green leaves. The branched heads of small white flowers are borne in early summer.

Cynara cardunculus
CARDOON
☼ 9-10 ↕ 5ft (1.5m) ↔ 4ft (1.2m)

The deeply divided, spiny, silver-gray leaves of this statuesque plant form big, bold clumps. During summer, stout blue flowerheads open on branched stems.

Dicentra 'Langtrees'
FRINGED BLEEDING HEART
☀ 4-8 ↕ 12in (30cm) 18in (45cm)

A charming plant with mounds of ferny, silver-blue leaves topped in late spring and early summer by nodding clusters of white flowers. It forms patches in time.

Galanthus caucasicus
SNOWDROP
☼ ☀ 3-9 ↕6in (15cm) ↔3in (8cm)

This vigorous snowdrop has broad, blue-green leaves and nodding white flowers with green-marked inner segments. It will eventually form large colonies.

EVERGREEN PERENNIALS WITH SILVER OR BLUE-GRAY FOLIAGE

Artemisia 'Powis Castle', see p.20
Festuca glauca 'Elijah Blue'
Heuchera 'Pewter Veil'
Lavandula angustifolia
Santolina chamaecyparissus
Sedum spathulifolium 'Cape Blanco'
Stachys byzantina 'Big Ears'
Tanacetum argenteum
Thymus pseudolanuginosus
Yucca glauca

Helictotrichon sempervirens
BLUE OAT GRASS
☼ 4-9 ↕5ft (1.5m) ↔24in (60cm)

A striking, evergreen grass forming a bold clump of stiff, narrow, gray-blue leaves. A sheaf of erect stems bears panicles of tiny spikelets above the leaves in summer.

Hosta 'Blue Moon'
HOSTA
☀ 3-9 ↕4in (10cm) ↔12in (30cm)

This slow-growing hosta is worth waiting for with its attractive clump of bloomy, heart-shaped, blue-green leaves. Racemes of nearly white flowers open in summer.

Lysimachia ephemerum
LOOSETRIFE
☼ ☀ 7-9 ↕3ft (1m) ↔12in (30cm)

The erect stems of this fine perennial are densely clothed in willowy, bloomy, sea green leaves. Slender spires of small white flowers are produced in summer.

HERBACEOUS PERENNIALS WITH SILVER OR BLUE-GRAY FOLIAGE

Achillea 'Moonshine'
Artemisia schmidtiana 'Nana'
Eryngium yuccifolium
Hosta 'Hadspen Blue', see p.67
Lychnis flos-jovis
Macleaya cordata
Nepeta spp. and cvs.
Perovskia atriplicifolia
Rudbeckia maxima
Thalictrum aquilegiifolium

Verbascum olympicum
OLYMPIC MULLEIN
☼ 6-8 ↕6ft (2m) ↔24in (60cm)

This stately, silvery, white-woolly biennial or perennial has a rosette of overwintering leaves. Tall, branched stems bearing dense spikes of yellow flowers appear in summer.

Perennials with Purple, Red, or Bronze Foliage

WHEN USED SELECTIVELY in garden plantings, perennials with unusual deep purple, bronze, or red foliage can provide a striking contrast among plants with lighter green, gray, or even yellow leaves. In some perennials, like *Cimicifuga simplex* 'Brunette', the color is long-lasting or even permanent, while in others it is mainly a spring display created by newly emerging foliage and stems. Sometimes the rich leaf color is also attractively overlaid by a lovely pale bloom, as is the case in several sedums.

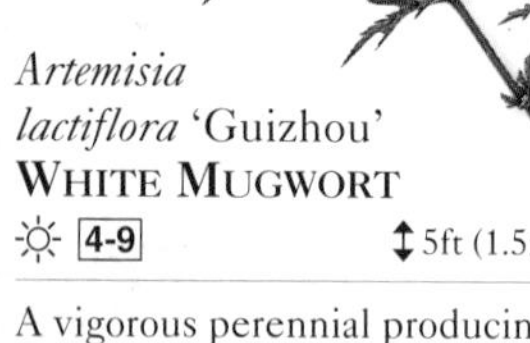

Artemisia lactiflora 'Guizhou'
WHITE MUGWORT
☼ 4-9 ↕5ft (1.5m) ↔3ft (1m)

A vigorous perennial producing clumps of branching, dark purple-flushed stems and deeply cut leaves. Sprays of tiny white flowers open from summer into autumn.

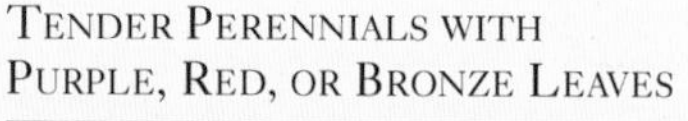

TENDER PERENNIALS WITH PURPLE, RED, OR BRONZE LEAVES

Canna 'Red King Humbert'
Coleus 'Molten Lava'
Cordylene australis 'Purpurea'
Dahlia 'Bishop of Llandaff', see p.104
Dahlia 'Ellen Houston'
Euphorbia amygdaloides 'Purpurea'
Pennisetum setaceum 'Rubrum', see p.134
Phormium tenax 'Purpureum'
Tradescantia pallida 'Purpurea'

Heuchera 'Rachel'
CORAL BELLS
☼ ◐ 3-8 ↕24in (60cm) ↔18in (45cm)

This striking plant forms a low clump of large, crinkled and lobed, shiny, bronze-purple leaves, purple beneath. Sprays of tiny, off-white flowers open in summer.

Cimicifuga simplex 'Brunette'
KAMCHATKA BUGBANE
◐ 3-8 ↕4ft (1.2m) ↔24in (60cm)

This superb perennial has clumps of large, divided, purplish brown leaves. Arching stems bear tall racemes of purple-tinted white flowers above the foliage in autumn.

Euphorbia dulcis 'Chameleon'
SPURGE
☼ ◐ 4-9 ↕↔12in (30cm)

The branching, purplish stems bear small red-purple leaves that color richly in autumn. Clouds of yellow, purple-tinted flowers appear in summer. It self-seeds.

Imperata cylindrica 'Rubra'
JAPANESE BLOOD GRASS
☼ ◐ 5-9 ↕16in (40cm) ↔12in (30cm)

An attractive grass with erect, leafy shoots and long green leaves that turn a deep blood red from the tips down. In summer, it bears sprays of silver-white spikelets.

Ophiopogon planiscapus 'Nigrescens'
MONDO GRASS
☼ ☀ 5-9 ↕ 8in (20cm) ↔ 12in (30cm)

Low tufts of narrow, leathery, black-purple leaves form patches in time. It has slender purple-white flower sprays in summer. An excellent evergreen groundcover.

Phormium 'Dazzler'
NEW ZEALAND FLAX
☼ 9-11 ↕ 3ft (1m) ↔ 4ft (1.2m)

This flax has stout clumps of evergreen, arching, strap-shaped, leathery leaves, impressively striped red, orange, and pink on a bronze-purple background.

Ranunculus ficaria 'Brazen Hussy'
LESSER CELANDINE
☼ ☀ 4-8 ↕ 2in (5cm) ↔ 6in (15cm)

The small rosettes or patches of long-stalked, heart-shaped, glossy, chocolate-brown leaves are an ideal backing for the shining, golden yellow flowers in spring.

Sedum 'Matrona'
SEDUM
☼ 5-9 ↕ 24in (60cm) ↔ 12in (30cm)

From late summer into autumn, flattened heads of starry pink flowers rise on stout, fleshy, purple-red stems above the robust clumps of fleshy, bloomy purple leaves.

Rodgersia podophylla
RODGERSIA
☼ ☼ 5-7 ↕ 5ft (1.5m) ↔ 6ft (1.8m)

Bronze-red when young, the large clumps of long-stalked, deeply divided and lobed leaves color red again in autumn. White flower plumes are borne in summer.

HERBACEOUS PERENNIALS WITH PURPLE, RED, OR BRONZE LEAVES

Anthriscus sylvestris 'Ravenswing'
Clematis recta 'Purpurea'
Foeniculum vulgare 'Purpureum', see p.119
Heuchera micrantha var. *diversifolia* 'Palace Purple'
Lobelia 'Queen Victoria'
Penstemon digitalis 'Husker Red'
Sedum telephium 'Arthur Branch'
Tiarella cordifolia 'Brandywine'

Sedum 'Sunset Cloud'
SEDUM
☼ 5-9 ↕ 10in (25cm) ↔ 18in (45cm)

One of the best of the low-growing purple sedums, it has fleshy, trailing or lax stems, bloomy foliage, and flattened pink flower-heads in late summer and autumn.

Perennials with Richly Tinted Autumn Foliage

All too often when we think of autumn color in the garden we look to woody deciduous plants like maples or sumacs. It is worth remembering that many herbaceous perennials, like those below, also produce a burst of bright color before the onset of winter.

Other Perennials with Richly Tinted Autumn Foliage

Aruncus aethusifolius, see p.119
Athyrium filix-femina, see p.140
Ceratostigma plumbaginoides, see p.44
Euphorbia griffithii 'Fireglow', see p.84
Geranium macrorrhizum, see p.83
Hosta ventricosa
Imperata cylindrica 'Rubra', see p.132
Miscanthus sinensis 'Purpurascens'
Osmunda regalis, see p.61
Polygonatum odoratum

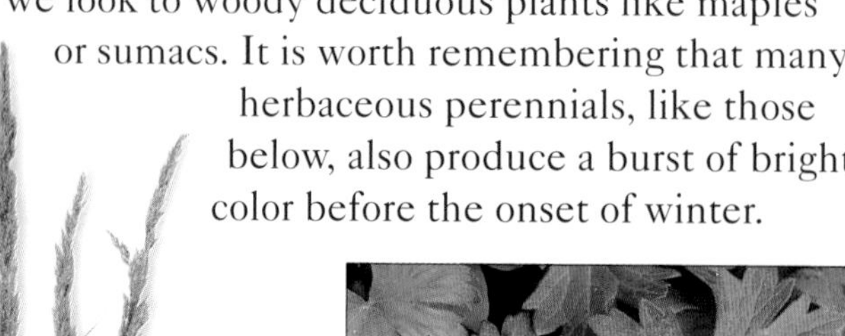

Geranium wlassovianum
Cranesbill
☼ ◐ 4-8 ↕↔ 24in (60cm)

The clumps of long-stalked, deeply lobed, velvety leaves emerge pinkish bronze in spring. They turn red with purple-bronze in autumn. Purple summer flowers.

Schizachyrium scoparium
Little Bluestem
☼ 3-10 ↕ 3ft (1m) ↔ 12in (30cm)

The dense tufts of arching, grayish green leaves and stems of this native grass turn purple to orange-red in autumn. Narrow, whiskery flower spikes appear in summer.

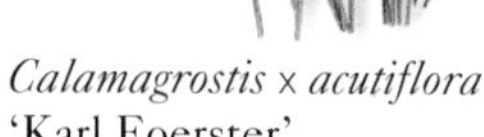

Calamagrostis × acutiflora 'Karl Foerster'
☼ ◐ 5-9 ↕ 6ft (1.8m) ↔ 24in (60cm)

This striking, clump-forming ornamental grass has stiffly erect stems and arching leaves. The pinky bronze spikelets turn a warm buff or pale brown in autumn.

Darmera peltata 'Nana'
Umbrella Plant
☼ ◐ 5-7 ↕ 14in (35cm) ↔ 24in (60cm)

Like the full-size umbrella plant, this dwarf form has rounded leaves that turn red or orange-copper in autumn. Leafless stems bear clusters of pink spring flowers.

Pennisetum setaceum 'Rubrum'
Fountain Grass
☼ 9-11 ↕ 3ft (1m) ↔ 24in (60cm)

Grown as an annual in the north, this spectacular grass forms a clump of erect, rich purple stems and leaves. The arching pink spikelets fade to pink-buff or white.

Sedum aizoon
Aizoon Stonecrop
☼ 4-9 ↕↔ 18in (45cm)

In autumn, the clumps of erect, reddish stems and fleshy, coarsely toothed leaves turn red or orange-red. Flattened heads of starry yellow flowers open in summer.

Perennials with Decorative Winter Foliage

IF PERENNIALS WITH RICHLY TINTED FOLIAGE in autumn are useful in the garden, then those with decorative foliage in winter are invaluable. When many plants have either died down or lost their leaves, these perennials will brighten up borders and beds. Several have yellow- or white-variegated leaves; others red-suffused, silver-hairy, or marbled foliage.

Arum italicum 'Marmoratum'
ITALIAN ARUM
6-9 ↕ 12in (30cm) ↔ 10in (25cm)

A reliable and eye-catching winter foliage plant with shiny arrow-shaped, cream-veined leaves. It produces greenish white flowers in early spring and red fall berries.

Bergenia 'Ballawley'
BERGENIA
4-9 ↕ 24in (60cm) ↔ 18in (45cm)

The low clumps of leathery, glossy green leaves turn rich bronze-purple in winter. In spring, upright red stems carry clusters of bell-shaped crimson flowers.

Celmisia semicordata
NEW ZEALAND DAISY
7-9 PH ↕ 20in (50cm) ↔ 12in (30cm)

Gray-green above and silvery beneath, the sword-shaped, silky-hairy leaves form a bold rosette. Gray-downy stems bear large daisylike flowerheads in summer.

Cyclamen coum Pewter Group
HARDY CYCLAMEN
5-9 ↕ 3in (8cm) ↔ 4in (10cm)

A beautiful selection of an early-spring flowering cyclamen with kidney-shaped, silvered leaves, often marked with dark green. Red-pink flowers add to its charm.

Epimedium × rubrum
RED EPIMEDIUM
4-8 ↕↔ 12in (30cm)

The clumps of much-divided leaves, red flushed when young, become red-tinted in autumn. Evergreen in southern zones. Spring flowers are crimson and yellow.

OTHER PERENNIALS WITH DECORATIVE WINTER FOLIAGE

Armeria maritima 'Rubrifolia'
Asplenium scolopendrium 'Crispum', see p.141
Carex morrowii 'Variegata'
Helleborus argutifolius, see p.114
Heuchera 'Chocolate Veil'
Lunaria annua 'Variegata'
Ophiopogon japonicus 'Nanum'
Polystichum acrostichoides
Vinca minor 'Variegata'

Sasa veitchii
HARDY BAMBOO
5-10 ↕ 5ft (1.5m) ↔ indefinite

This vigorous, creeping bamboo has bold, evergreen leaves that wither at the edges in autumn, giving them decorative white margins for winter. It needs lots of space.

Specialist Plants

Certain perennials are now some of the most enthusiastically collected garden plants. Valued for their foliage, flowers, or form, their increasing availability is making it easier than ever to create a unique plant collection.

Polystichum munitum for moisture or shade

△ Hellebores *Excellent groundcovers,* Helleborus x hybridus *seedlings are some of the most desirable perennials.*

Imagine a garden filled with 100 different hardy geraniums, or 50 assorted peonies, or even a great multitude of hardy ferns. In fact, there are many such gardens, and they are increasing in number as collecting members of a single genus or family continues to catch gardeners' imaginations. Collecting has appealed to plantsmen and women in Europe for the last 400 years at least, and for many centuries more in China and Japan. In recent years, it has become very popular in North America as well.

The perennials in this section are among the most sought-after plants. Some, such as hostas and hardy geraniums, have long been popular, with numerous cultivars already available, and many more introduced each year. Others, like ornamental grasses, which have the combined attraction of elegant habit, foliage, and seedheads, and hellebores and epimediums, have been "discovered" more recently, but are now avidly collected.

Mix and Match

While the search for as many selections of a particular perennial as possible can be a mixture of fun and adventure, the entire garden does not have to be filled with just one plant and its variations. If you are selective, choosing only the best plants, or those that appeal to you, it is possible to combine a collection of a particular perennial with other garden plants to provide varied, year-round appeal.

Establishing a Collection

So many different perennials are available that it is easy to establish a collection to suit the size and situation of your garden. Sedums or saxifrages, for example, can be grown in a small urban backyard using troughs or containers, and if your chosen plants are large shrubs or bush roses, groundcovers such as hardy geraniums can be grown beneath them. Given the right garden conditions, a number of collections can be established together: hardy ferns, snowdrops, pulmonarias, and epimediums will all thrive in each other's company.

△ Peonies *Famed for their foliage and flowers, classics like* Paeonia x smouthii *will make a striking show in the garden.*

◁ Geraniums *Justifiably popular and very easy to grow, geraniums are perfect for ground cover, or for borders and beds.*

▷ Mixed Grasses *When planted for contrasting effect, as here, ornamental grasses can make a spectacular collection.*

Small Grasses and Sedges

LONG NEGLECTED, perennial grasses and sedges are now being rediscovered and increasingly cultivated for their ornamental value. Ideal for smaller gardens, those suggested below will make a striking addition to borders or good specimen plants.

Carex muskingumensis
PALM SEDGE
☼ ◐ 4-9 ↕ 24in (60cm) ↔ 18in (45cm)

With its loosely tufted habit, erect, leafy shoots, and horizontally spreading leaves, this native sedge resembles a miniature palm tree or a bamboo.

OTHER SMALL GRASSES AND SEDGES

Carex conica 'Variegata'
Festuca glauca 'Sea Urchin'
Imperata cylindrica 'Rubra', see p.132
Miscanthus sinensis 'Yaku Jima'
Pennisetum alopecuroides 'Little Bunny'
Stipa tenuissima, see p.71

Deschampsia cespitosa 'Goldschleier'
TUFTED HAIR GRASS
☼ ◐ 4-9 PH ↕↔ 3ft (1m)

During summer, slender shoots bearing showers of tiny green spikelets that mature a bright silvery yellow rise above the clumps of narrow, evergreen leaves.

Festuca glauca 'Blaufuchs'
BLUE FESCUE
☼ 4-9 ↕ 12in (30cm) ↔ 10in (25cm)

Good for contrast, this is one of the best small, blue-leaved grasses. Its name, 'Blue Fox', aptly describes the dense tufts of narrow, bright blue leaves and stiff shoots.

Pennisetum orientale
FOUNTAIN GRASS
☼ 7-9 ↕ 24in (60cm) ↔ 30in (75cm)

A superb specimen plant forming a dense, neat mound of narrow leaves. The arching shoots carry spikes of soft, long-bristled, pink-tinted spikelets during summer.

Carex siderosticha 'Variegata'
BROAD-LEAVED SEDGE
☼ ◐ 6-9 ↕ 12in (30cm) ↔ 16in (40cm)

One of the most ornamental sedges with a creeping habit excellent for ground cover. Its arching, strap-shaped, white-margined leaves form a low, dense mound.

Elymus magellanicus
WILD RYE
☼ 5-9 ↕ 24in (60cm) ↔ 12in (30cm)

Both the tufts of long, slender leaves and the shoots that carry narrow flower spikes in summer are an intense, almost electric, blue. Excellent as a specimen plant.

Stipa tenuifolia
FEATHER GRASS
☼ 7-9 ↕ 24in (60cm) ↔ 30in (75cm)

This graceful grass forms dense clumps of long, slender, bright green leaves. It bears arching, feathery plumes in summer. Ideal for combining with other perennials.

Large Ornamental Grasses

Grown as specimens in a lawn or in a bed underplanted with smaller perennials, these bold grasses can create a grand spectacle, especially in late summer or autumn when in flower. They are all easy to grow and can be planted singly or in groups for a more immediate effect.

Calamagrostis brachytricha
Reed Grass
☼ ◐ 5-9 ↕ 4ft (1.2m) ↔ 3ft (1m)

Dense clumps of erect shoots bear narrow heads of purplish spikelets in late summer or autumn. Excellent for winter effect, the spikelets later turn a warm brown.

Cortaderia selloana 'Sunningdale Silver'
☼ 8-11 ↕ 10ft (3m) ↔ 8ft (2.5m)

A big, bold, evergreen pampas grass with sturdy stems bearing large, silvery white plumes that last well into winter. This is a popular and well-proven cultivar.

Other Large Grasses

Andropogon gerardii
Arundo donax 'Macrophylla', see p.116
Chasmanthium latifolium, see p.70
Miscanthus sacchariflorus
Miscanthus sinensis 'Silberfeder'
Miscanthus sinensis 'Zebrinus', see p.125
Stipa gigantea

Chionochloa conspicua
Plumed Tussock Grass
☼ 6-9 ↕ 6ft (2m) ↔ 3ft (1m)

Graceful, branched heads of creamy white spikelets, maturing pale silver-brown, rise on tall shoots in summer above the clump of evergreen, reddish brown-tinted leaves.

Cortaderia richardii
Toe Toe
☼ 7-9 ↕ 10ft (3m) ↔ 6ft (2m)

Tall shoots extend from the mound of arching, evergreen leaves during summer to flaunt graceful, drooping, creamy white, shaggy plumes that persist into winter.

Miscanthus sinensis 'Cabaret'
Miscanthus
☼ 5-9 ↕ 6ft (1.8m) ↔ 4ft (1.2m)

Conspicuous white stripes line the leaves of this attractive, clump-forming grass. In autumn, it bears feathery copper-hued flowerheads that rise above the foliage.

Ferns for Moisture or Shade

OF ALL NON-FLOWERING PERENNIALS, ferns are easily the most garden-worthy, offering an exciting variety of shapes and heights for use as specimen plants or in bold groupings. Most of the following ferns are of medium to large size and will thrive given humus-rich soil, moisture, and shade.

Asplenium scolopendrium
HART'S TONGUE FERN
5-9 ↕↔ 24in (60cm)

This bold fern is easily recognized by its long, leathery, strap-shaped, evergreen fronds, marked beneath with stripes of brown spores. It is fond of alkaline soil.

OTHER FERNS FOR MOISTURE OR SHADE

Dryopteris affinis
Dryopteris goldieana
Dryopteris filix-mas
Matteuccia struthiopteris, see p.65
Osmunda cinnamomea
Osmunda regalis, see p.61
Polystichum acrostichoides
Polystichum braunii

Athyrium filix-femina
EUROPEAN LADY FERN
4-8 ↕ 4ft (1.2m) ↔ 24in (60cm)

The feathery, finely divided, light green fronds form a graceful clump with a green or red-brown central stalk. It is especially good for waterside sites.

Dryopteris erythrosora
AUTUMN FERN
5-8 ↕↔ 24in (60cm)

One of the most colorful of hardy ferns, its coppery red young fronds in spring and summer contrast with the overwintering, shiny, dark green, mature fronds.

Dryopteris wallichiana
WALLICH'S WOOD FERN
5-8 ↕ 36in (90cm) ↔ 30in (75cm)

The erect fronds of this lovely fern form a big, semievergreen clump and have dark-scaly stalks. Its fronds will grow much taller if rich soil and shelter are provided.

Polystichum munitum
WESTERN SWORD FERN
6-9 ↕ 36in (90cm) ↔ 4ft (1.2m)

Once it is established this luxuriant fern can transform an otherwise dull corner or border. Its laddered, evergreen fronds will form a large, handsome clump.

Polystichum polyblepharum
JAPANESE TASSEL FERN
5-8 ↕ 24in (60cm) ↔ 36in (90cm)

The distinctive clump of prickle-toothed, much-divided fronds is covered at first with golden hairs. It is especially effective when planted with other ferns.

Polystichum setiferum
SOFT SHIELD FERN
5-8 ↕ 4ft (1.2m) ↔ 36in (90cm)

This graceful and beautiful fern develops a large, loose clump of semievergreen, finely divided, dark green fronds. It will thrive in a shady rock garden.

Ferns for Walls and Crevices

FERNS THAT PREFER growing in the crevices of rocks and cliffs in the wild are mostly small to very small in size. They can be established in similar situations in the garden – in damp stone walls where space between the stones allows – or they may be used as charming container or trough plants.

Asplenium adiantum-nigrum
BLACK SPLEENWORT
8-9 ↕6in (15cm) ↔8in (20cm)

A tough little evergreen fern with wiry black stalks and triangular, much-divided, leathery, shiny green fronds. It thrives in alkaline soils.

Asplenium ceterach
RUSTY-BACK FERN
7-9 ↕5in (12.5cm) ↔10in (25cm)

This species forms a tuft of strap-shaped, deeply lobed, scaly-backed, evergreen fronds that curl in times of drought, and recover again after rain.

OTHER FERNS FOR WALLS AND CREVICES

Asplenium viride
Blechnum penna-marina
Cheilanthes feei
Cheilanthes tomentosa
Cystopteris fragilis
Pellaea atropurpurea
Polypodium vulgare 'Cornubiense', see p.115

Asplenium ruta-muraria
WALL RUE SPLEENWORT
4-7 ↕4in (10cm) ↔5in (12.5cm)

Often found growing with *A. trichomanes* in the wild, this fern forms dense colonies of small, much-divided, leathery, evergreen fronds. It is fond of alkaline conditions.

Asplenium scolopendrium 'Crispum'
HART'S TONGUE FERN
5-9 ↕20in (50cm) ↔24in (60cm)

The strap-shaped, wavy-margined, shiny, fronds of this attractive evergreen fern gradually form a bold clump. Also ideal for the front of a shady border.

Asplenium trichomanes
MAIDENHAIR SPLEENWORT
2-9 ↕6in (15cm) ↔8in (20cm)

Delicate-looking but tough, this little fern produces an evergreen rosette of slender, black-stalked fronds with neatly paired divisions. It prefers alkaline conditions.

Polypodium cambricum
Pulcherrimum Group
8-9 ↕18in (45cm) ↔24in (60cm)

The decorative, deeply divided, triangular to lance-shaped fronds have crested tips. The fronds emerge during the summer and stay fresh and green until late winter.

Woodsia polystichoides
HOLLY FERN WOODSIA
5-8 ↕8in (20cm) ↔10in (25cm)

One of the prettiest ferns for walls or rock crevices producing small clumps of lance-shaped, deeply divided, pale green fronds. It may be damaged by late spring frosts.

Tall, Vigorous Bamboos

THE LUSH INFORMALITY and glossy, evergreen foliage of these tall-growing bamboos make them excellent for screening, especially on moist, well-drained soils in sheltered sites. All can be extremely invasive. Their growth can be curbed effectively by planting them in containers.

Chimonobambusa quadrangularis
SQUARE-STEMMED BAMBOO
☀ 8-11 ↕ 6ft (5m) ↔ indefinite

The older canes of this very fast-growing bamboo are peculiarly four-angled and mature from green to brown. They carry large sprays of arching, shiny green leaves.

Pseudosasa japonica
SLASH BAMBOO
☼ ☀ 7-11 ↕ 20ft (6m) ↔ indefinite

A handsome bamboo commonly grown for screening. The heavy mass of striking green foliage forces the dense stands of green canes to arch at the tips in maturity.

Semiarundinaria fastuosa
NARIHIRA BAMBOO
☼ ☀ 6-9 ↕ 15ft (5m) ↔ 12ft (4m)

This stately, erect bamboo has purple-brown-striped canes with dense sprays of foliage. Clump-forming in cool climates, it spreads extensively in warmer areas.

OTHER TALL, VIGOROUS BAMBOOS

Phyllostachys aurea
Phyllostachys aureosulcata
Phyllostachys aureosulcata 'Spectabilis'
Phyllostachys dulcis
Phyllostachys nigra
Phyllostachys vivax 'Aureocaulis'
Pleioblastus simonii
Semiarundinaria yashadake
Yushania maculata

Phyllostachys viridiglaucescens
PHYLLOSTACHYS
☼ ☀ 7-11 ↕ 5m (16ft) ↔ indefinite

Like all *Phyllostachys* species, it produces pairs of branches from the cane joints. Large stands of green canes arch widely under the weight of its lush, glossy foliage.

Qiongzhuea tumidinoda
QIONGZU CANE
☀ 6-8 ↕ 15ft (5m) ↔ indefinite

Recently introduced from China, this bamboo with swollen cane joints is famous as a source of walking sticks. The sprays of narrow leaves turn yellow in full sun.

Yushania anceps
ANCEPS BAMBOO
☼ ☀ 8-10 ↕ 12ft (4m) ↔ indefinite

An excellent bamboo for screening that forms a dense thicket of slender, glossy canes. The arching to pendent branches are thickly clothed in fresh green foliage.

Clump-forming Bamboos

THERE ARE FEW MORE ELEGANT and impressive evergreen perennials than those bamboos that slowly increase to form single clumps of canes. They are best displayed as specimens in a sheltered lawn, bed, or woodland glade, and are lovely by water as long as they are not planted in wet soil.

OTHER CLUMP-FORMING BAMBOOS

Chusquea culeou 'Tenuis'
Fargesia denudata
Fargesia robusta
Himalayacalamus falconeri 'Damarapa'
Thamnocalamus crassinodus 'Kew Beauty'
Thamnocalamus spathiflorus

Chusquea culeou
FOXTAIL BAMBOO
6-9 ↕20ft (6m) ↔8ft (2.5m)

The densely packed, yellowish or green canes form an impressive, vase-shaped clump and look like foxtails with their clusters of branches crowded at each joint.

Fargesia nitida
FOUNTAIN BAMBOO

5-8 ↕15ft (5m) ↔10ft (3m)

This aptly named bamboo has a bold, dense clump of slender, arching, purplish canes, which mature to yellow-green and bear handsome showers of narrow leaves.

Fargesia murieliae
UMBRELLA BAMBOO
5-8 ↕12ft (4m) ↔10ft (3m)

An excellent specimen plant producing a vase-shaped clump of arching, bloomy white canes aging to green then yellow-green with large plumes of slender leaves.

Semiarundinaria yamadorii
SEMIARUNDINARIA
7-9 ↕10ft (3m) ↔6ft (2m)

Well-furnished with a mass of handsome, dense green foliage, this is a bamboo of real character and value. Its tall, narrow green canes form a dense, upright clump.

Thamnocalamus tessellatus
ZULU BAMBOO
7-9 ↕12ft (4m) ↔6ft (2m)

Conspicuous, papery white sheaths clothe the tall canes of this dense, clump-forming bamboo, giving them a banded effect. It was once used to make Zulu shields.

Geraniums for Collectors

HARDY GERANIUMS, or cranesbills as they are also called, are among the most popular of all perennials. This is partly because of their many uses in the garden, and partly because of their great variety of habit, foliage, and flowers. No garden should be without at least a few of the following.

Geranium himalayense 'Plenum'
LILAC CRANESBILL
☼ ☀ 4-8 ↕ 10in (25cm) ↔ 24in (60cm)

Also known as 'Birch Double', this pretty cranesbill is ideal for the front of a border. It has neatly divided leaves and loosely double, old-fashioned blooms in summer.

OTHER GERANIUMS FOR COLLECTORS

Geranium 'Brookside', see p.27
Geranium clarkei 'Kashmir Pink'
Geranium dalmaticum
Geranium x *magnificum*
Geranium x *riversleaianum* 'Russell Prichard', see p.100
Geranium sinense
Geranium wlassovianum, see p.134

Geranium 'Nimbus'
CRANESBILL
☼ ☀ 3-7 ↕ 16in (40cm) ↔ 24in (60cm)

This low-grower spreads by underground, creeping stems to form a mound of prettily divided leaves that are yellowish when young. It has purple-pink summer flowers.

Geranium 'Salome'
CRANESBILL
☼ ☀ 6-9 ↕ 12in (30cm) ↔ 6ft (2m)

The faintly marbled leaves of this low-grower are suffused yellow when young. Dusky violet-pink flowers with dark veins and eyes appear from summer to autumn.

Geranium sylvaticum 'Amy Doncaster'
WOOD CRANESBILL
☼ ☀ 3-8 ↕ 28in (70cm) ↔ 18in (50cm)

In summer, this lovely form of the wood cranesbill bears white-eyed, deep purple-blue flowers. It commemorates the plantswoman who first selected it in her garden.

Geranium kishtvariense
CRANESBILL
☼ ☀ 6-9 ↕ 12in (30cm) ↔ 24in (60cm)

Underground, creeping stems form a low patch of wrinkled, deeply lobed leaves. The brilliant pinkish purple, finely-lined flowers appear in summer and autumn.

Geranium phaeum 'Lily Lovell'
CRANESBILL
☼ ☀ 5-8 ↕ 32in (80cm) ↔ 18in (45cm)

A charming form of the mourning widow cranesbill producing attractively lobed, light green leaves. In summer, showers of mauve-purple, white-eyed flowers appear.

Geranium wallichianum
CRANESBILL
☼ ☀ 4-8 ↕ 12in (30cm) ↔ 36in (90cm)

The attractively lined, lilac-purple flowers of this carpeting cranesbill are borne over a long period during summer and autumn. Its marbled leaves are shallowly lobed.

Hostas for Collectors

The already bewildering number of hostas increases each year, with new variations in leaf shape, size, texture, and color, as well as the bonus of attractive flowers. Here is a selection of favorites for planting singly or in groups or drifts. Classic plants for shade, they are also handsome in containers.

Hosta 'Buckshaw Blue'
Hosta
☼ ☀ 3-9 ↕ 14in (35cm) ↔ 24in (60cm)

The heart-shaped, slightly "dished" leaves are boldly veined and beautifully bloomy, forming a striking clump. Nodding flowers open in short-stalked racemes in summer.

Hosta 'Golden Tiara'
Hosta
☼ ☀ 3-9 ↕ 12in (30cm) ↔ 20in (50cm)

One of the best small hostas, this forms a compact clump of heart-shaped, yellow-margined leaves. It produces tall racemes of lavender-purple flowers in summer.

Hosta gracillima
Hosta
☼ ☀ 4-9 ↕ 2in (5cm) ↔ 7in (18cm)

Charming for containers, rock gardens, or walls, this tiny hosta's spreading, narrow leaves have wavy margins. It bears slender spires of pinkish violet flowers in autumn.

Other Hostas for Collectors

Hosta fluctuans 'Variegated'
Hosta 'Great Expectations'
Hosta 'Inniswood'
Hosta 'Northern Halo'
Hosta 'Paul's Glory'
Hosta plantaginea 'Aphrodite'
Hosta 'Summer Fragrance'
Hosta tokudama 'Flavocircinalis'
Hosta 'Zounds', see p.60

Hosta hypoleuca
Hosta
☼ ☀ 4-9 ↕ 18in (45cm) ↔ 36in (90cm)

This attractive species has large, pale green leaves with a gray bloom above and striking, mealy-white undersides. It bears pale mauve to white flowers in summer.

Hosta lancifolia
Hosta
☼ ☀ 4-9 ↕ 18in (45cm) ↔ 30in (75cm)

Long grown in gardens, this hosta forms a loose clump of narrow, glossy, dark green leaves. It makes a good groundcover. In summer, racemes of purple flowers appear.

Hosta montana 'Aureomarginata'
Hosta
☼ ☀ 3-9 ↕ 28in (70cm) ↔ 36in (90cm)

Slow to establish but worth the wait, this superb specimen plant has long-stalked, large, shiny leaves with irregular, bright gold margins and white summer flowers.

Hosta tokudama
Hosta
☼ ☀ 3-9 ↕ 14in (35cm) ↔ 36in (90cm)

Beautiful but slow-growing, this hosta has pale mauve to white flowers in summer and forms a compact clump of rounded to heart-shaped, corrugated, glaucous leaves.

Snowdrops for Collectors

IF YOU ARE THRILLED BY THE SIGHT of a drift of common snowdrops in the late winter garden or in woodland, then prepare for a pleasant surprise. There are dozens of lesser known varieties of snowdrop, each with its own particular charm and characteristics, and most are very easy to cultivate.

Galanthus 'Augustus'
SNOWDROP
☀ 3-9 ↕6in (15cm) ↔3in (8cm)

This robust snowdrop has relatively wide, silver-channeled leaves and distinctly rounded, large flowers with green-tipped inner segments. It forms colonies in time.

OTHER SNOWDROPS FOR COLLECTORS

Galanthus 'Barbara's Double'
Galanthus 'Benhall Beauty'
Galanthus caucasicus 'Comet'
Galanthus 'Merlin'
Galanthus nivalis subsp. *imperati* 'Ginns'
Galanthus nivalis 'Lady Elphinstone'
Galanthus nivalis 'Sandersii', see p.98

Galanthus 'Magnet'
SNOWDROP
☀ 3-9 ↕8in (20cm) ↔3in (6cm)

The distinguished, scented flowers sway in the slightest breeze on their unusually long and slender stalks. This is one of the best and most reliable snowdrops.

Galanthus nivalis 'Scharlockii'
SNOWDROP
☀ 3-9 ↕↔4in (10cm)

This curious form of the common snowdrop has nodding, green-tipped flowers, with spathes split into two segments that stand above the blooms like rabbit's ears.

Galanthus 'Ophelia'
SNOWDROP
☀ 3-9 ↕6in (15cm) ↔8in (20cm)

A must for every collection, this very early snowdrop has fully double blooms on slender stalks. The outer segments have pinched tips, sometimes marked green.

Galanthus 'John Gray'
SNOWDROP
☀ 3-9 ↕6in (15cm) ↔3in (8cm)

Exquisite and early flowering, this is one of the most collectable snowdrops. It has pendent flowers carried on long, slender stalks, with inner segments marked green.

Galanthus 'Mighty Atom'
SNOWDROP
☀ 3-9 ↕5in (12cm) ↔3in (8cm)

An outstanding, easily grown snowdrop bearing attractive, slender-stalked flowers with inner segments that are distinctively stained green at their tips.

Galanthus reginae-olgae
SNOWDROP
☼ 6-9 ↕4in (10cm) ↔3in (8cm)

The earliest-flowering snowdrop, usually blooming in autumn before its green, silver-channeled leaves emerge. It is slow to increase, growing best in a sunny site.

Hellebores for Collectors

HELLEBORES ARE AMONG the most fashionable and collectable perennials for partially shaded sites in the garden. A wealth of named selections is rapidly becoming available, especially from China, while the range of hybrids and mixed garden seedlings already offered is enormous.

Helleborus atrorubens
HELLEBORE
5-9 ↕12in (30cm) ↔18in (45cm)

A choice species with circular, deeply divided, long-stalked leaves, often purple-tinted when young. Its starry, late winter flowers vary from deep purple to green.

Helleborus lividus
HELLEBORE
7-9 ↕18in (45cm) ↔12in (30cm)

Silver-veined, evergreen leaves, tinted pink beneath, are accompanied by apple-green, pink-flushed flowers in winter. Best grown in an alpine house in cold areas.

Helleborus multifidus subsp. *hercegovinus*
HELLEBORE
6-9 ↕12in (30cm) ↔18in (45cm)

Best known for the lacy effect of its finely dissected leaves, this hellebore also bears attractive, yellowish or pale green flowers during late winter or early spring.

Helleborus odorus
HELLEBORE
6-9 ↕↔20in (50cm)

This showy, easy-to-grow species is free-flowering, with masses of scented, green to yellow-green flowers in late winter or early spring. A bold, clump-forming plant.

OTHER HELLEBORES FOR COLLECTORS

Helleborus argutifolius 'Pacific Frost'
Helleborus dumetorum
Helleborus niger 'Potter's Wheel', see p.99
Helleborus orientalis
Helleborus purpurascens
Helleborus torquatus
Helleborus viridis subsp. *occidentalis*

Helleborus x *sternii* 'Boughton Beauty'
HELLEBORE
6-9 ↕↔20in (50cm)

In late winter, green-tinted pink flowers are borne above the mound of evergreen, beautifully veined and marbled, grayish leaves. Needs protection in cold areas.

Helleborus torquatus Party Dress Group
HELLEBORE
6-9 ↕16in (40cm) ↔12in (30cm)

A delightful, if unusual, group of small hellebores that produces multi-petaled flowers in a variety of colors from winter to early spring before the leaves emerge.

Helleborus versicarius
HELLEBORE
6-9 ↕18in (45cm) ↔12in (30cm)

This curious but desirable hellebore bears small, cupped, green-and-purple blooms in late winter and early spring followed by inflated pods. It is dormant in summer.

Epimediums for Collectors

THE INTRODUCTION OF MANY NEW SPECIES from China has elevated epimediums to among the most collectable perennials. As woodland plants with attractive deciduous or semievergreen foliage, they make excellent groundcovers. Once established, they will thrive in a dry, shady site.

Epimedium acuminatum
EPIMEDIUM
☼ 6-9 ↕ 18in (45cm) ↔ 30in (75cm)

A magnificent, clump-forming evergreen with large, lance- or arrow-shaped leaflets and long-spurred, pale purple, or purple and white flowers in spring and summer.

Epimedium davidii
EPIMEDIUM
☼ 5-8 ↕ 12in (30cm) ↔ 18in (45cm)

The dark, shining stems of this choice epimedium species bear semievergreen, divided leaves and nodding, long-spurred yellow flowers from spring into summer.

OTHER EPIMEDIUMS TO COLLECT

Epimedium franchetii
Epimedium grandiflorum 'Lilafee'
Epimedium grandiflorum f. *violaceum*
Epimedium x *perralchicum* 'Wisley'
Epimedium pinnatum subsp. *colchicum*, see p.46
Epimedium pubigerum
Epimedium x *versicolor* 'Sulphureum'
Epimedium x *warleyense*

Epimedium grandiflorum
'Rose Queen'
☼ 4-8 ↕ 12in (30cm) ↔ 18in (45cm)

The heart-shaped, prickle-toothed leaflets form a low mound and are prettily tinted when young. Showers of long-spurred, deep rose-pink flowers open in spring.

Epimedium leptorrhizum
EPIMEDIUM
☼ 6-9 ↕ 10in (25cm) ↔ 18in (45cm)

In time, this creeping evergreen develops patches of stems with attractively veined, prickle-toothed leaflets. Its long-spurred flowers open in spring and early summer.

Epimedium x *perralchicum*
'Fröhnleiten'
☼ 5-8 ↕ 16in (40cm) ↔ 24in (60cm)

Worth growing for its foliage alone, as the prickle-toothed, glossy, dark green leaves are beautifully bronze-tinted when young. Pendent spring flowers are bright yellow.

Epimedium stellulatum 'Wudang Star'
EPIMEDIUM
☼ 5-8 ↕ 16in (40cm) ↔ 12in (30cm)

Multitudes of small, starry white flowers, with bold yellow beaks, are borne on wiry stems in spring above the heart-shaped, prickle-toothed, shiny, evergreen leaflets.

Epimedium x *versicolor* 'Versicolor'
EPIMEDIUM
☼ 4-8 ↕↔ 12in (30cm)

This is a real charmer with its low clump of semievergreen foliage, red-tinted when young. The loose sprays of yellow, pink-suffused flowers also open in spring.

Peonies for Collectors

WILD HERBACEOUS PEONIES, bearing their simple, usually single blooms of fragile petals and gold stamens, never fail to bring a touch of elegance to the garden. Although their flowering period is relatively brief, they often have decorative foliage that extends their value in the garden.

Paeonia cambessedesii
MAJORCAN PEONY
☼ 7-8 ↕22in (55cm) ↔24in (60cm)

This very distinctive peony has purple- and red-flushed stems and shiny, metallic gray-green leaves that are red or purple beneath. It spring flowers are rose-pink.

OTHER PEONIES TO COLLECT

Paeonia clusii
Paeonia japonica
Paeonia obovata
Paeonia obovata var. *alba*
Paeonia peregrina 'Otto Froebel'
Paeonia potaninii
Paeonia tenuifolia 'Rosea'
Paeonia veitchii var. *woodwardii*
Paeonia 'White Wings'

Paeonia mascula subsp. *arietina*
PEONY
☼ ☀ 5-8 ↕30in (75cm) ↔24in (60cm)

This stout clump-former has handsome, deeply divided, grayish green leaves and bears bowl-shaped, reddish pink flowers with creamy yellow stamens during spring.

Paeonia x *smouthii*
PEONY
☼ ☀ 4-8 ↕↔28in (70cm)

A little-known but reliable hybrid that forms clumps of finely divided leaves and produces fragrant, cup-shaped, bright red blooms in late spring and early summer.

Paeonia tenuifolia
PEONY
☼ 5-8 ↕↔18in (45cm)

Quite unlike any other species, this forms bold clumps of beautiful, finely dissected leaves. The cupped, deep red flowers are borne in late spring and early summer.

Paeonia emodi
HIMALAYAN PEONY
☼ ☀ 6-8 ↕↔32in (80cm)

In late spring, slightly nodding, cupped, fragrant white flowers are carried by the handsome clump of branched stems with deeply divided leaves. Enjoys a shady site.

Paeonia mlokosewitschii
CAUCASIAN PEONY
☼ ☀ 5-8 ↕↔28in (70cm)

This well-known peony has stout clumps of downy, gray-green leaves. Its lemon-yellow blooms in late spring and summer are followed by bright red seed capsules.

Paeonia wittmanniana
PEONY
☼ ☀ 5-8 ↕↔36in (90cm)

An outstanding species with bold clumps of glossy, dark green leaves. Bowl-shaped, pale yellow flowers, borne from late spring to summer, are followed by red seed pods.

Index

Plants that are illustrated in the book are indicated by this symbol ▦

A

B

F

G

H

I

JK

L

O

PQ

R

S

T

Acknowledgments

AUTHOR'S ACKNOWLEDGMENTS
Once again, I am indebted to my wife Sue who somehow made time in a busy life to decipher and type my handwritten notes for this book. My thanks also to Hatton Gardner for checking the index, and to David Barker, Joyce Cama, Cliff Dad, Dilys Davies, Pat Jackson, Danae Johnston, Chris Mortimer, Bob Mousley, and Ray Wilson of the Hardy Plant Society, who kindly helped with suggestions, as did Sarah Drew, Jean Fletcher, Hala Humphries, Sabine Liebherr, and George Smith. Beyond these few are the many who have encouraged my interest in perennials over the years. To all of you, my heartfelt thanks. Last but certainly not least, my editorial team, initially Lesley Malkin and Colin Walton, but principally Anna Cheifetz and Helen Robson, who must have sweated at times over my schedule but remained calm and focused throughout. Thanks for your patience, guidance, and gentle prodding.

DORLING KINDERSLEY would like to thank Howard Rice for all his additional help, Ann Kay for proof reading, Lesley Malkin and Colin Walton for their support and initial work on this project, Simon Maughan, and Richard Hammond.

PHOTOGRAPHY CREDITS
Key: l=left, r=right, t=top, c=center, b=bottom
Commissioned photographs: Howard Rice, Colin Walton, and Andrew Henley; **additional pictures:** Clive Boursnell, Deni Bown, Jonathan Buckley, Andrew Butler, Eric Crichton, Andrew de Lory, Christine Douglas, John Fielding, Neil Fletcher, John Glover, Derek Hall, Jerry Harpur, Sunniva Harte, Neil Holmes, Andrew Lawson, Howard Rice, Robert Rundle, Juliette Wade, Colin Walton, Matthew Ward, and Steven Wooster.
Agency photographs: Garden Picture Library: John Glover 2, 12br, 88tr, 136bl; Steven Wooster 14br, 42bl, 113; **Jerry Harpur** (designer: Sheila McQueen): 9b; **Andrew Lawson** (designer: Wendy Lauderdale): 14bl; **Scope Features:** Steve Poole 8tr; **Derek St Romaine:** 11tr; **Howard Rice:** 4, 9tr, 10bl, 10br, 11tl, 13tl, 13tr, 13br, 15, 27bm, 27tr, 39br, 42br, 43, 70tl, 70bl, 70bm, 70br, 71bm, 71tr, 88bl, 88br, 89, 97bm, 112bl, 112tr, 134bl, 137; **Roy Lancaster:** 8bl, 22tl, 22bl, 24bl, 30bl, 30tc, 31tr, 36tr, 38tr, 40br, 64tl, 76tr, 83bm, 98bl, 102tm, 11bm, 118tr, 123tm, 123bm, 127tr, 128mr, 133mm, 134bl, 134bm, 135tr, 136tr, 139br, 142bm, 143tl, 147br, 148ml, 148tm, 148mr; **Matthew Ward:** 10tl, 12ml (containers by Malcolm Hillier).

PHOTOGRAPHERS' ACKNOWLEDGMENTS
In England: Alan Shipp, Beth Chatto Gardens, Bressingham Gardens, Broadlands Gardens, Cambridge Alpines, Cambridge Bulbs, Cambridge Garden Plants, Cambridge University Botanic Gardens, David Austin Roses Ltd., Fulbrooke Nursery, Goldbrooke Plants, Hadlow College, Hopleys Plants Ltd., John Morley, Langthorns Plantery, Monksilver Nursery, Paradise Centre, Peter Lewis, Potterton and Martin, Rickard's Hardy Ferns, Mrs. Sally Edwards, West Acre Gardens. **In Australia:** Birchfield Herbs (Marcia Voce), Buskers End (Joan Arnold), Elizabeth Town Nursery (John and Corrie Dudley), Essie Huxley, Garden of St. Erth, Island Bulbs (Kevin Fagan, Viv Hale), Lambley Nursery (David Glenn), Moidart Wholesale Nursery (Graham Warwick), Otto Fauser, Penny Dunn, Rosevears Nursery (Rachael Howell) Sally Johansohn, Suz Price, Theresa Watts, Woodbank Nursery (Ken Gallander), Yates.

USDA Hardiness Zone Map

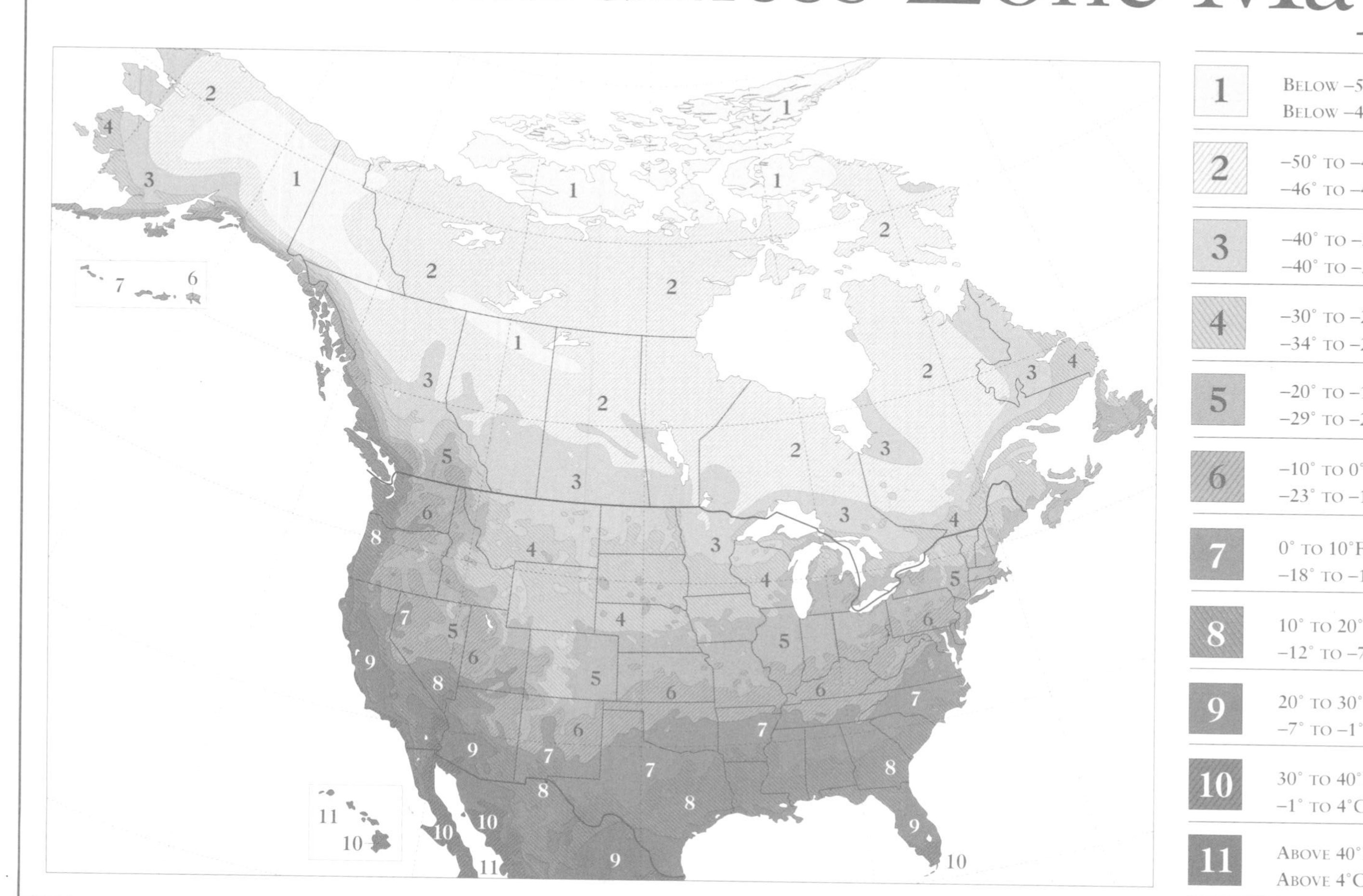

Zone	°F	°C
1	Below –50°F	Below –46°C
2	–50° to –40°F	–46° to –40°C
3	–40° to –30°F	–40° to –34°C
4	–30° to –20°F	–34° to –29°C
5	–20° to –10°F	–29° to –23°C
6	–10° to 0°F	–23° to –18°C
7	0° to 10°F	–18° to –12°C
8	10° to 20°F	–12° to –7°C
9	20° to 30°F	–7° to –1°C
10	30° to 40°F	–1° to 4°C
11	Above 40°F	Above 4°C